The Journal of the History of Philosophy Monograph Series
Edited by Richard A. Watson and Charles M. Young

John Craige's
Mathematical Principles
of Christian Theology

Richard Nash

Published for
The Journal of the History of Philosophy, Inc.

SOUTHERN ILLINOIS UNIVERSITY PRESS
Carbondale and Edwardsville

94 93 92 91   4 3 2 1

Library of Congress Cataloging-in-Publication Data

Nash, Richard, 1955–
John Craige's Mathematical principles of Christian theology / by
Richard Nash.
p.   cm. — (Journal of the history of philosophy monograph
series)
"Published for the Journal of the History of Philosophy, Inc."
Includes English translation of Craig's Theologiæ christianæ
principia mathematica.
Includes bibliographical references.
1.   Craig, John, d. 1731. Theologiæ christianæ principia
mathematica. 2.   Eschatology—History of doctrines—18th century.
3.   Theology—Methodology—History of doctrines—18th century.
4.   Probabilities. 5.   Religion and science—History—18th century.
I.   Craig, John, d. 1731. Theologiæ christianæ principia
mathematica. English. 1991. II.   Title. III.   Series.
BT820.N37   1991
230'.01'51—dc20   89-39678
ISBN 0-8093-1662-5   CIP

To
Berta Sturman
and
Ralph Nash
With infinite gratitude, uniformly increasing

The algebraic theology of Craig.
What is one to think of this?

Samuel Beckett, Molloy

CONTENTS

The *Journal of the History of Philosophy*
Monograph Series
xi

Acknowledgments
xiii

Introduction
xv

1. Responses to Craige's *Theology*
1

2. John Craige's Life
8

3. Mathematical Principles of the *Theology*
19

4. Intellectual Context of the *Theology*
32

Appendix
The Mathematical Principles of Christian Theology
49

Notes
84

Works Cited
90

Index
93

THE *JOURNAL OF THE HISTORY OF PHILOSOPHY*
Monograph Series

THE *JOURNAL OF THE HISTORY OF PHILOSOPHY* MONOGRAPH SERIES, CONSISTing of volumes averaging 80 to 120 pages, accommodates serious studies in the history of philosophy that are between article length and standard book size. Editors of learned journals have usually been able to publish such studies only by truncating them or by publishing them in sections. In this series, the *Journal of the History of Philosophy* presents, in volumes published by Southern Illinois University Press, such works in their entirety.

The historical range of the *Journal of the History of Philosophy* Monograph Series is the same as that of the *Journal* itself—from ancient Greek philosophy to the twentieth century. The series includes extended studies on given philosophers, ideas, and concepts; analyses of texts and controversies; new translations and commentaries on them; and new documentary findings about various thinkers and events in the history of philosophy.

The editors of the Monograph Series, the directors of the *Journal of the History of Philosophy,* and other qualified scholars evaluate submitted manuscripts.

We believe that a series of studies of this size and format fulfills a genuine need of scholars in the history of philosophy.

Richard A. Watson
Charles M. Young
—Editors

ACKNOWLEDGMENTS

THIS PROJECT HAS TAKEN SHAPE OVER A LONG PERIOD OF TIME. IN BOTH THE research and the writing I have incurred numerous obligations, the greatest of which I happily acknowledge here. Dennis Todd, Ralph Nash, Doug Patey, Hugh Culik, and Matthew Pass all offered assistance and encouragement when it was most needed. A trip to England to work with important archival material was facilitated by a Summer Faculty Fellowship from Indiana University, and made especially pleasant by Linda and Kaye Teasley's hospitality. Throughout the research for this project, I have required access to a variety of archives, rare book and manuscript collections. That work has been considerably eased in a variety of ways by the (often anonymous) assistance of librarians at San Diego State University Library; the Houghton Library of Harvard University; the University of Michigan Library; the Burton Historical Collection of the Detroit Public Library; the New York Public Library; the National Union Theological Seminary, Cambridge University Library; the Portsmouth Collection, Wren Library, Trinity College, Cambridge; the Bodleian Library, Oxford University; Christ Church College Library, Oxford University; Edinburgh University Library; the National Library of Scotland, Edinburgh; the British Library, London; and the Public Record Office, London. Through it all, Nancy Rutkowski has been both my most critical reader and my most supportive friend. Finally, I owe a special "thank you" to my most unabashedly enthusiastic supporter, Carolyn Nash, who unselfishly sent me off to work every evening after dinner.

INTRODUCTION

THIS WORK OF HISTORICAL RECOVERY ATTEMPTS TO SITUATE IN ITS CONTEXT a rare early attempt to introduce mathematical reasoning into moral and theological dispute. An appendix makes available to scholars for the first time an English language version of the complete *Mathematical Principles of Christian Theology*. The opening chapter charts the wide range of responses elicited by the work. Chapter 2 presents a more complete biography of the author than currently exists, introducing new material and correcting several widely reproduced errors of fact. Subsequent chapters locate the work and its responses within a context of profound intellectual change occurring at the end of the seventeenth and the beginning of the eighteenth centuries, paying particular attention to mathematical and philosophical contexts. As an older notion of probability came to be replaced by our modern one, the two competing notions existed for a time side by side, engendering confusion and enflaming controversy. This work helps identify that process of historical change.

A brief pamphlet that sold for sixpence, the *Theology* was printed only once in Craige's lifetime. Like most of Craige's work, it was written in Latin and relied on a mathematical argument. The *Theology,* however, attracted a broader audience than did the rest of his work. Patterning his effort on Newton's discovery of the mathematical principles of natural philosophy and elaborating on hints found in Locke's *Essay on Human Understanding* and *The Reasonableness of Christianity,* Craige attempted to introduce mathematical reasoning to problems in Christian theology. Foremost among these problems was the declining faith in Christianity and the corresponding rise in atheism and deism that then so preoccupied the established Church. Borrowing Locke's notion of "an historical faith" (*Reasonableness* 101), Craige developed several rules for the evaluation of historical evidence in an attempt to explain this phenomenon. His treatise attempted at once to account for the declining faith in Christianity while answering the millenarian claims of enthusiasts. One result of his efforts was to draw down upon himself the responses of deists, clergymen, mathematicians, historians, philosophers, and poets. These responses, from an audience scattered from Edinburgh to Padua, continued long after Craige's death in 1731 and included, among many others, such notable figures as Matthew Tindal, Samuel Clarke, Humphrey Ditton, Phillipe Montmort, William Warburton, David Hume, and Alexander Pope.

The various positions adopted by participants in the controversy surrounding this work reveal conflicting assumptions about the nature of belief and demonstration. Recent studies of the emergence of a modern notion of probability at the end of the seventeenth century point to a profound intellectual shift governing the determination of belief, as private reason and the testimony of the senses challenge the authority of external testimony. Michel Foucault's archaeological inquiry claims to reveal what he terms a discontinuity between epistemes at this time, with a new system of signs emerging as the basic structure of Western thought: "It was this system that introduced into knowledge probability, analysis, and combination and the justified arbitrariness of the system" (63). Ian Hacking, in what has been termed "an investigation in the style of Michel Foucault, although a great deal more clear" (Anne M. Fagot qtd. in "From the Emergence of Probability," 106), has explored the philosophical shifts that were required before an inductive theory of probability logic could emerge. Barbara Shapiro documents the confusion between conflicting notions of probability across the spectrum of seventeenth-century thought. Douglas Lane Patey, arguing against Hacking that the emergence of probability was not properly an intellectual revolution, but an evolution, proceeds to chart the important role of the emergent notion in Augustan literature and literary criticism. The competing assumptions of the various responses to the *Theology* indicate the jostling that took place as an older notion of probability gave way to the new; at the same time, the range of responses Craige's work elicited testifies to how widely felt this conflict was.

The same limitations that may undermine its value as moral philosophy tend to underline its importance to intellectual history. By restoring to Craige's treatise and its responses a legitimacy and respect denied by nineteenth-century historians, we gain a richer perspective on the assumptions and ideologies, conflicts and controversies that marked the end of the seventeenth and the beginning of the eighteenth centuries. The emotional intensity with which Craige's arguments were rejected, often without a reasoned critique, by a wide range of respondents suggests a fundamental anxiety surrounding the role of belief.

For Pascal and the early developers of probability logic who followed him, probability theory offered a tool as well suited to moral as to mathematical calculations. Practitioners often sought a mathematical guide to distinguish between the roles of chance and design in the governance of the world. Although Craige's treatise has most often been discussed in this context as an early contribution (of dubious value) to the emerging field of probability theory, Craige was in fact working out of a background in the geometrical foundations of the equally new field of the calculus of fluents. In the history of the fluxional calculus, he has earned a small but established reputation. Craige was one of the very first in England to comprehend the power of the new mathematics, and his publications made him a leader in developing the calculus and introducing the now standard Leibnizian notation in place of the Newtonian dot notation to England.

Craige's reliance on the geometrical tools of the new calculus of fluents rather than on the induction of probability reveals a fundamental conflict over the nature of mathematical demonstration during the period. Drawing on Charles S. Peirce's distinction between "induction" and "abduction," between "decision under uncertainty" and generating principles subject to experimental verification (qtd. in Hacking, *Emergence* 75), it becomes possible to recognize two quite distinct attitudes toward probability reasoning: an essentially fideist view motivating the inductivist approach followed by Pascal being resisted by a more rationalist view that informed the abductive approach Craige adopted.

This fundamental conflict is underlined by observing that Craige's last four chapters—which present a demonstration of Pascal's "wager" argument—are drawn not from Pascal, but from John Locke's restatement of that argument. Although Locke was aware of the mathematical theory of probability formulated by Pascal, he nowhere alludes to it in his writings. The reason for this lies in his ideas concerning the value of mathematical demonstration. For Locke, the power of mathematics consists of deductive demonstrations that result in certain knowledge; he does not recognize the validity of an inductive mathematics whose results cannot guarantee exactness. The absence of the probability calculus in the works of Locke and Craige is not evidence of their ignorance, but rather testimony to their rejection of its inductive method as insufficient. They would consider the versions of the wager argument they offer more valid than that presented by Pascal, precisely because they avoid his doctrine of chances in favor of a Newtonian method of deductive demonstration proceeding from universally acknowledged hypotheses.

It has been easy to mock the *Theology,* and I would be the last to claim that the work is not bizarre. Yet modern accounts that dismiss the work as a "travesty" of Pascal's wager (Hacking, *Emergence* 72) fall into the same error as Lubbock and Drinkwater in the nineteenth century who dismissed the work as "an insane parody of Newton's *Principia*" (45). The ad hominem assumption behind these appraisals—that Craige was at best an eccentric, and at worst a fool—does not hold up under examination. A significant (though minor) mathematician, Craige adopts a legitimate (though long misunderstood) skeptical view of probability reasoning.

In attempting to treat his work and the issues surrounding it seriously and to sort out the confusion that accompanied ideas of probability, we are forced to confront—and to a degree, modify—modern theories of the history of probability reasoning. Where Hacking and Patey argue that Locke "had no conception of probability logic" (Hacking, *Emergence* 70), I try to show that (like Craige) he consciously avoids endorsing the inductive method. Instead, both Locke and Craige advocate a Newtonian method that analyzes particular events, generalizes by careful induction to a hypothesis, and from such principles derives a demonstration through deductive reasoning. The purpose of such a method was to keep the use of induction to a minimum and use hypotheses only so long as they could be confirmed experientially.

In pursuing this work I have profited much from the research of both recent and traditional historians, and I hope I have been able to draw successfully from each. Throughout, my goal has been one of historical recovery, investigating and making accessible a rare work that in this century has been more often discussed than read. I have sought to combine biographical and bibliographical scholarship—uncovering evidence not in the public record, and correcting several widely reproduced errors of fact—with critical and historical analysis of the work's mathematical and philosophical argument. In this enterprise, I have been influenced by a common line of analysis shared by what Steven Shapin has termed "new contextualism" in the history of science (96) and what Stephen Greenblatt has termed "new historicism" in the history of literature (5): I have sought, not to construct a historical background against which to read Craige's text, but to allow Craige's text to speak for itself in defining its relationship to the context in which it occurs. In doing so, I have sought to correct both of the easy misconceptions currently available regarding this work. Neither a "travesty" of Pascal's wager, nor "an insane parody of Newton's *Principia*," Craige's work appears anomolous in terms of its relationship both to Pascal's doctrine of chances and Newtonian geometry. Only by understanding its relationship to both can we come to understand the larger philosophical issues at work in its production.

This project should interest historians and students of the period, especially those interested in the history of mathematics. Stephen Stigler's recent argument that the *Theology* presents an early viable model of calculating inverse probabilities should considerably stimulate interest in this translation. Beyond this audience, however, this study necessarily addresses issues of significance to students of religion and philosophy of the period. In recent years, the emergence of probability has become a subject of theoretical interest to scholars in philosophy, literature, and history as a potential instance of the kind of paradigm shift that characterizes fundamental intellectual change.

John Craige's
Mathematical Principles
of Christian Theology

1

Responses to Craige's *Theology*

In May of 1699, Timothy Childe, bookseller, first published John Craige's *Theologiae Christianae Principia Mathematica*.[1] The thirty-six page pamphlet was available at the White Hart in St. Paul's Churchyard for the moderate price of sixpence. This little treatise with the imposing title could hardly have excited much popular attention, for it was not reissued. Today, few people are aware either of Craige (1663?–1731) or of the *Theology,* and discussions of the work often echo the judgment of Lubbock and Drinkwater in the nineteenth century:

> 76. It is not necessary to do more than mention an essay, by Craig, on the probability of testimony, which appeared in 1699, under the title "Theologiae Christianae Principia Mathematica." This attempt to introduce mathematical language and reasoning into moral subjects can scarcely be read with seriousness; it has the appearance of an insane parody of Newton's Principia, which then engrossed the mathematical world. . . .
> 77. An anonymous essay in the Philosophical Transactions of the same year, and of not much greater value, may perhaps be attributed to the same author.[2] (45)

In this century, Florian Cajori, in his *History of Mathematics,* dismisses the work as "an absurd abuse of mathematics in connection with the probability of testimony" (171). In *A History of the Study of Mathematics at Cambridge,* W. W. Rouse Ball paid it a backhanded compliment: "It is, however, much easier to obtain a lasting reputation by eccentricity than by merit; and hundreds who never heard of Craig's work on fluxions know of him as the author of *Theologia[e] Christianae Principia Mathematica* published in 1699" (78).

This remains Craige's reputation today, although the *Theology* has received more attention in the past twenty-five years than in the preceding two hundred. An anonymous translation of portions of the first two chapters dealing with his general algorithm for the diminution of the credibility of historical evidence was published as "Craig's Rules of Historical Evidence" in 1964. Two recent works by Hacking in 1975 and Patey in 1984 have done much to open up discussion concerning the origins of probability, but have discussed the work briefly (and for the most part, disparagingly) under the influence of earlier judgments. A more recent discussion of Craige's argument by Stigler in 1985 is both more thorough and more sympathetic. Most recently, Lorraine Daston has briefly but sensitively located Craige's treatise in an emerging concern with the relationship between mathematical probability and psychological belief. Yet even Stigler's attempt to rehabilitate Craige's reputation by discerning in his argument an extraordinarily early anticipation of modern statistical analysis qualifies its endorsement by noting that "at first glance [his] definitions seem more than vague, they suggest that we are reading the work of a crank" (4). If, however, it is easy to dismiss the argument of Craige's treatise, it is due less to individual eccentricity than to the *Theology* being a document very much of and for a particular time. The limitations that undermine its value as moral philosophy underline its importance to intellectual history. By restoring to Craige's treatise and its responses a legitimacy and respect denied by the nineteenth century, we may gain a richer perspective on the assumptions and anxieties, conflicts and controversies that marked the end of the seventeenth and the beginning of the eighteenth centuries.

The *Theology* contains two arguments—the first spanning two chapters, the second four—loosely connected by their attempt to introduce geometrical demonstration into moral philosophy. The argument of the last four chapters is generally held to have been written first and consists of a geometrical demonstration in the tradition of Pascal's wager, heavily influenced by Locke.[3] The reputation of the *Theology* has always been shaped by the argument of the first two chapters, which contain an algorithm for measuring the diminution of credibility with specific application to religious faith. Craige argues that any historical account, whether transmitted orally or in writing, suffers from diminishing credibility relative to three external variables: the number of times the account is transmitted, the distance an account is removed from the original event, and the time elapsed from the original event. Developing a function to describe this change and applying it to the text of the Gospel, Craige attempts to show mathematically that faith in the history of Christ, as it depends on written testimony, will not disappear before the year 3150. Then, taking his text from Luke 18:8, "When the Son of man returns, will he find no faith on Earth?," Craige concludes that 3150 is the earliest possible date of the Apocalypse.

One may be tempted to agree with Lubbock and Drinkwater's easy assessment of such a work as "an insane parody"; any attempt to predict mathematically the end of the world is sufficiently strange to call its status into question. The work, however, is neither a parody nor insane, and in some respects it is more typical than aberrant. Indeed, the essay "of the same year, and of not much greater value" that they erroneously attribute to Craige suggests that there existed a ready audience for such works and that others besides Craige explored the subject. "A Calculation of the Crediblity of Human Testimony," which appeared anonymously in *Philosophical Transactions of the Royal Society* in November 1699, was written by George Hooper, later Bishop of Bath and Wells. A footnote by the editor of Hooper's *Works* in 1757 points out Hooper's earlier use of a similar calculation in his "Discourse on Lent," written in 1685 and published in 1689 (127). The work has been correctly attributed to Hooper by the editors of the *Dictionary of National Biography*, by the nineteenth-century theologian Convers Francis in a manuscript note attached to the Houghton Library's copy of the *Theology*, by Brown Grier in an unpublished essay cited by Stigler, and most recently by Daston, who was the first to discuss the obvious mathematical differences between Craige's work and Hooper's, yet in most histories of probability the misattribution cited by Todhunter still enjoys wide circulation (see, for example, Patey). Hooper's essay was in fact quite distinct from Craige's, and as we shall see below, it was a direct response to Craige's work. Nor were these two alone in their discussion of the subject. In 1699, Samuel Bradford's Boyle Lectures (the most popular forum for moral philosophy at the time) presented rational arguments, as the title page announced, for "the Credibility of the Christian Revelation." The next year Bradford delivered a ninth sermon, subsequently published as an appendix to the Boyle Lectures, "in reply to an objection." Without recourse to mathematical argument, Bradford argued that belief in the Gospel is "reasonable and fitting." Craige was in good company in his basic concern with developing rational arguments about belief.

Two premises underlie Craige's argument. The first is that belief is not fixed and compelled, but is subject to change; the second is that the further we are removed from an event through time and space, the greater are the suspicions we entertain concerning reports of that event. All of the attacks on the *Theology* concern these premises.

Throughout the eighteenth century, mathematicians, theologians, and philosophers returned to a problem that lies at the heart of Craige's treatise: Can one develop a rigorous model for measuring the credibility of human testimony? According to Todhunter, in 1701, Johann Wilhelm Petersen (1649–1727) published his *Animadversiones* against Craige's *Theology*, and while Petersen accepted the substance of Craige's argument, he invoked a different law of diminution to arrive at the less comforting prediction that 1789 would be the year of the Apocalypse.[4] Petersen was a Lutheran theologian in Germany who published a number of treatises, including several on the Apocalypse. Samuel Clarke's Boyle Lecture of 1705, *A Discourse on the Evidence of Natural and Revealed Religion*, addressed the same issue. Clarke knew Craige, and his phrasing suggests that he had Craige's treatise in mind throughout his discussion:

The chief Evidence of the Facts on which the Truth and Certainty of the Christian Revelation depends, to *Us who live Now at this distance of Time,* is the *Testimony of our Saviour's Followers;* which in all its Circumstances, was the most credible, certain, and convincing Evidence, that was ever given to any Matter of Fact in the World. . . . It is very certain, that the Apostles' Testimony concerning the Works and Doctrine of Christ, is *truly and without corruption conveyed down to Us,* even unto this Day. . . . So that there is no room or possibility of any considerable *corruption,* such as might in any wise diminish our certainty of the Truth of the whole. (379–86)

In 1712, Humphrey Ditton, a respected mathematician and Newtonian theologian, confronted the same problem in his *Discourse Concerning the Resurrection of Jesus Christ.* His response to Craige formed the basis for most subsequent attacks. John Edwards, a High Church Tory divine, vehemently attacked Craige's treatise in 1714 as "a most scandalous and prophane attempt" in *Some New Discoveries of the Uncertainty, Deficiency, and Corruption of Human Knowledge and Learning:*

There is a late *Algebraic* writer, who undertakes to prove, that *there is only a Probability of the Truth of the Christian Religion, and that the Christian Faith is only a Perswasion, that such and such Propositions are true, because they are probable. There is not, there cannot be, any Certainty in Christianity. . . .*
    And a great Parcel of Definitions, Axioms, Theorems, Lemma's [sic] and Scholiums, is produced to prove this. Yet notwithstanding all this great Parade, it is demonstratively evident, that his Assertion is groundless and false; for in the very Nature of the Thing it self, it is plain, that the Degree of Probability of our Saviour's History will not be lessen'd, but increas'd and strengthen'd; because there will be an accession to these degrees continually. (85–86)

Borrowing heavily from Ditton and echoing the conclusion of Edwards, the Abbé Houtteville believed he thoroughly refuted Craige in *La Religion Chrétienne Prouvée par les Faits* in 1722, even showing that the testimony of succeeding witnesses, far from diminishing probability, actually adds to the credibility of an event. He suggested of Craige that "his opinion is the greatest example of the vanity of human conjecture"(335).[5]

Matthew Tindal specifically rejected Craige's argument in 1730 in his famous *Christianity as Old as Creation* where he writes of "a Reverend Divine [who has fixed] the precise time, when all probability of the truth of the history of Christ will be entirely spent and exhausted"(163). Two years later, Bishop Berkeley also denied Craige's claims concerning the declining credibility of the Gospel, both in the sixth dialogue of *Alciphron, or the Minute Philosopher* (2:313) and in his "Sermon Preached Before the Society for the Propagation of the Gospel" (4:399). William Warburton began his *Divine Legation of Moses* of 1738 by discussing "internal" and "external" evidence. He contends that external evidence "must therefore become more and more imperfect, without being affected by that whimsical and partial calculation, to which a certain *Scotchman* would subject it" (2). In the following year, David Hume addressed Craige's argument in his *Treatise of Human Nature:*

> 'Tis from the original impression, that the vivacity of all the ideas is deriv'd, by means of the customary transition of the imagination; and 'tis evident this vivacity must gradually decay in proportion to the distance, and must lose somewhat in each transition. . . . But as it seems contrary to common sense to think that if the republic of letters and the art of printing continue on the same footing as at present, our posterity, even after a thousand ages, can ever doubt if there has been such a man as JULIUS CAESAR; this may be considered as an objection to the present system. . . . From this topic there has been borrow'd a very celebrated argument against the *Christian Religion.* (144–45)

Hume's refutation at once rehearses the arguments of Ditton and Houtteville and serves as the basis for Alexander Pope's subsequent attack on Craige in the fourth book of the *Dunciad.* When Hume anonymously published his *Treatise* in 1739 refuting Craige's "celebrated argument," he had sent a copy to Pope. Any celebrity the *Theology* enjoyed in 1739 was certainly augmented three years later when Pope enshrined Craige in the *Dunciad* in the character of the "gloomy Clerk," with an accompanying refutation that echoes Hume:

> Be that my task (replies a gloomy Clerk,
> Sworn foe to Myst'ry, yet divinely dark;
> Whose pious hope aspires to see the day
> When Moral Evidence shall quite decay.
> (4:459–62)

Although these lines are often glossed as a punning reference to the better-known Samuel Clarke, Pope's own footnote identifies Craige as the figure he has principally in view:

> Alluding to a ridiculous and absurd way of some Mathematicians, in calculating the gradual decay of Moral Evidence by mathematical proportions: according to which calculation, in about fifty years it will be no longer probable that Julius Caesar was in Gaul, or died in the Senate House. See *Craig's Theologiae Christianae Principia Mathematica.* But as it seems evident, that facts of a thousand years old, for instance, are now as probable as they were five hundred years ago; it is plain that if in fifty more they quite disappear, it must be owing, not to their Arguments, but to the extraordinary Power of our Goddess; for whose help therefore they have reason to pray. P.W. (54.459n)

Thus, forty years after its publication and eleven years after its author's death, Craige's *Theology* became the source of the only known instance of David Hume's direct influence on Alexander Pope.

In 1755, J. Daniel Titius published a second edition of the *Theology* in Leipzig, accompanied by a critical preface almost as long as the treatise itself, in which he notes that while Craige's later works employ the Newtonian method of fluxions, his early works credit Leibniz rather than Newton with the development of the calculus: "After Craige as a young man had quite properly followed in the footsteps of Leibniz, using his method and notation, he would deserve more praise if later, as an old man following Newton with equal intensity (and towards a fellow countryman too), he had not replaced the name 'differential' with 'method of fluxions'"(14).[6] In addition to many of the responses already noted, Titius devotes considerable space to Craige's reception on the continent, citing the reactions of Abraham-Gotthelf Kaestner (1719–1800), Giovanni Poleni (1683–1761), Jacques Hermann (1678–1733), François-Antoine Knittel (1721–92), Henri Guillaume Clemm (1725–75), Gustave, Comte de Bonde (1682–1764), and Phillipe Montmort (1678–1719). Montmort's response in 1710 in his *Essai D'Analyse* stands out, not simply because he was the most gifted mathematician to respond to Craige, but because (and perhaps there is a connection) he alone managed to balance skepticism concerning Craige's undertaking with respect and even a degree of admiration for the argument:

> I believe that it is impossible to estimate the probability that is to be given to the testimony of man, either transmitted orally or in writing. Nevertheless, it is that which has been undertaken by a learned English Geometer, whose honest and obliging manners have prejudiced me in favor of his heart as much as his excellent works have for their genius. The book of which I speak has for its title: *Philosophiae [sic] Christianae Principia Mathematica*. Mr. Craig is the author. This work is too curious not to say something of it here. The author there proposes to himself principally to prove against the Jews the truth of the history of Jesus Christ, and to demonstrate to the Libertines that the course they take of preferring the pleasures of the world is so slight and of such short duration when compared even to the uncertain hope of the benefits promised to those who will follow the laws of the gospel, that it is not a reasonable course nor conformable with their true interests. Mr. Craig has doubtless well understood that all these consequences can only be true by virtue of an arbitrary supposition of a distance which may in truth be half that, or a third, or a fourth, etc. I say may be, because what way is there of knowing? He would be able by making other hypotheses, equally likely, to find very different numbers. For myself, I find the design of Mr. Craig laudable and pious and his execution as successful as it could be; but I believe this work is much more proper to exercise Geometers than to convert Jews or unbelievers. What one is able to conclude after reading this work is that the author is very clever, that he is an impressive Geometer, and that he has much wit.[7] (xxxvii)

Montmort's balance of skepticism and respect stands in stark contrast to the vehement responses the *Theology* more typically provoked. Indeed, the emotional intensity with which Craige's arguments were rejected, often without a reasoned critique, suggests a fundamental anxiety surrounding the role of belief. The work provoked emotional responses across the theological spectrum: skeptics, deists, papists, dissenters, and both High and Low Church Anglicans. Craige himself, a clergyman in the Church of England, addresses his argument against "atheists and deists" (Appendix 53); yet of all his respondents, only the deist Tindal seems to accept that he is writing in opposition to, rather than in support of, deism.

The attention that the *Theology* demanded and the controversy that it provoked resulted from its concern with the nature of belief. In his preface Craige describes the nature of belief:

> For faith is nothing other than that persuasion of the mind, derived from an indeterminate probability, by which we believe certain propositions to be true. If the persuasion arises from certainty, then it is not faith that is being produced, but knowledge. Probability generates faith, but destroys knowledge; certainty, on the other hand, generates knowledge and destroys faith. Thus, knowledge removes every occasion for doubt, while faith leaves always a certain hesitation in the mind. (Appendix 54)

Implicit in Craige's discussion is an axiomatic need for certainty. Moreover, in the discussion surrounding Craige's *Theology,* no one takes issue with Craige's attempt to remove that "certain hesitation in the mind"; rather, they argue with Craige's method for removing that hesitation. What emerges from the debate is an anxiety of uncertainty with participants attempting to reconcile the certainty of knowledge with the doubt that accompanies belief. At the extreme poles of this debate were the rational positivists, who saw no limit to the possibilities of rational demonstration, and the most enthusiastic Protestants, who submitted to the certainty of absolute faith.

In discussing the *Theology* and its place in Augustan thought, we need to go beyond simply evaluating its argument; we need to understand its terms, methods, and assumptions. How does Craige's use of a mathematical framework relate to the mathematical theories of probability and the calculus? How and why do Craige's terminology and methods of argument echo and alter those of Pascal, Locke, and Newton? How do Craige's arguments and their responses reflect a more widespread anxiety concerning the relationship of faith and reason? Some of the confusion and anxieties underlying responses to the work may be clarified by focusing on the author. Even a brief examination of his life reveals that far from the image conjured up by Lubbock and Drinkwater of a mentally unbalanced eccentric laboring in isolation, Craige was an ordinary man of more than ordinary intellect whose contributions to mathematics (while modest) were not insignificant and whose abilities were respected and remarked upon by some of the most noted figures of the day.

2

John Craige's Life

WE KNOW RELATIVELY LITTLE ABOUT CRAIGE'S EARLY LIFE AND FAMILY.[1] HE
was born in Scotland late in 1662 or early in 1663, the second son of the vicar
of Hoddam in the county of Dumfries. The exact date of birth is unknown and
the parish registers are lost. His father, James (c. 1632–1704), took his M.A.
from Edinburgh University on 23 May 1655 and was ordained vicar of Hoddam
in 1661. The family moved first to Selkirk in 1666 when James was translated to
that living, and they moved again in 1676 when he obtained the living at Tranent.
Craige appears to have been a descendant of John Craig, the Scottish reformer,
and thus a distant relative of Bishop Gilbert Burnet, who was the great-grandson
of Sir Thomas Craig.[2] The earliest recorded incident in Craige's life is a rather
puzzling connection with Burnet. According to an account given by Thomas
Burnet in the "Life" of his father, prefaced to the 1724 edition of the Bishop's
History of My Own Times, Craige was living in London with Gilbert Burnet in
1674, when Burnet was thirty and Craige only twelve. Thomas Burnet says he
has this information from "the Rev. Mr. John Craig" (xxi), but does not explain
the circumstances. Except for this item, Craige's early years are a blank.

In 1678, John's older brother, William (c. 1657–1720/21), matriculated at
Edinburgh; he received his M.A. in 1680. The following year, James was deprived of the living at Tranent for refusing to submit to the Sacramental Test.[3]
For six years he was without a church living until he was installed vicar of the
Canongate in 1687. In 1683, David Gregory (then still a student) succeeded his
uncle, James Gregory, as professor of mathematics at Edinburgh. The following
year John Craige matriculated and began studying under Gregory, forming a
friendship that would last a lifetime. Craige's credentials as a mathematician were
established early; by the age of twenty-six, he would count among his friends
and associates David Gregory, Archibald Pitcairne, Colin Campbell, Colin Mac-
Laurin, Robert Hooke, Edmond Halley, and Isaac Newton.

In 1685, Craige interrupted his studies in order to journey to Cambridge and
publish his first work, *Methodus Figurarum Lineis Rectis et Curvis Comprehensarum Quadraturas Determinandi* (*A Method for Determining the Quadratures*

8

of Figures Determined by Straight Lines and Curves). The work was one of the first in England to exploit the new method of the calculus, and it was the first English work to use the Leibnizian notation *dx* and *dy* used today in place of the Newtonian dot notation. In the work, Craige acknowledges the influence of Leibniz, Newton, and especially Isaac Barrow. Throughout his career, Craige seems to have been particularly influenced by Barrow, and portions of the *Theology* (especially chapters 3–6) seem to follow closely Barrow's *Geometrical Lectures*.

This trip to Cambridge marked the emergence of Craige as one of a small group of mathematicians at work on the sophisticated problems surrounding the emergence of the calculus. While in Cambridge, Craige met Isaac Newton and became one of a handful of men to read over Newton's work on the calculus in manuscript. Craige appears to have remained on good terms with Newton throughout his life. Newton's library contains copies of all Craige's works (including the *Theology*), and on the death of Newton, his nephew, John Conduitt, solicited a memorial from Craige for a memoir that was never published. In his *De Calculo Fluentium*, Craige refers to the initial visit:

> You have here, gentle reader, my thoughts about the calculus of Fluents. The first elements of this I thought over when I was a young man about the year 1685. At that time, while I was living in Cambridge, I asked the most worthy Mr. Newton if he would kindly read through them before I committed them to the press. This in his great humanity he did, and to corroborate some objections raised in my pages against D. D. T[schirnhaus], he willingly offered to me the quadratures of two figures: these were the curves whose equations were $m^2y^2 = x^4 + a^2x^2$, and $my^2 = x^3 + ax^2$ At the same time, he informed me that he was able to exhibit innumerable curves of this kind through an *infinite series*, which, by breaking off under given conditions, gave a geometric quadrature of the proposed figure. Later, on returning to my homeland I became very friendly with the most learned physician, Mr. Pitcairne, and with Mr. D. Gregory, to whom I signified that Mr. Newton had such a series for quadratures, of which each of them admitted to being wholly unaware.[4](2)

Working from the two equations given to Craige and accurately discerning their sequence, Gregory was soon able to recover Newton's general theorem, and he told Pitcairne and another mathematician, Colin Campbell, of the "discovery" (Newton, *Correspondence* 2:451).[5] When the news got back to Craige that Gregory had adopted the formula as his own, he wrote to Newton requesting a copy of Newton's full theorem. When the theorem arrived, it proved identical to Gregory's, which Craige hastened to point out. Although Craige was too late to prevent Pitcairne from publishing the theorem as Gregory's discovery, he may have succeeded in virtually suppressing the work, for the tract is very rare today. In a letter to his friend Campbell, Craige hardly disguises his surprise and dismay at Pitcairne's conduct:

For your further satisfaction, [I promise to send you] Mr. Newton's Series for
Quadratures, which he was pleased to send me in a letter not long since (I must tell
you by the by that I saw this Series at Cambridge & acquainted Dr. Pit & Mr. Greg:
with it, & told them the chiefe propertie of it, *sc*: that it breaks off when the figur's
Quadrable. At which time they were altogether ignorant of such a series as I can let
you see by letters of the Dr: written to me at Cambridge; which astonished me to
find no mention made of Mr. Newton by the dr: but keep this to your selfe). (Newton,
Correspondence 3:8–9)

Newton had shown Craige not only the two equations that he took back to
Scotland, but most of his papers pertaining to the calculus, including *De Analysi*.[6]
In Craige's copy of the first edition of the *Principia,* there are numerous additions
in the margin "taken from the Author's Copy intended for a second edition"
(Cohen 204).[7] The Scholium to Proposition 34 (35 in the first edition), Theorem
28, Book 2 reads in part, "This Proposition I conceive may be of use in the
building of ships" (Newton, *Philosophiae* 1:474).[8] Next to this, Craige has
written, "The occasion for this afterthought I myself provided, when in Cambridge
I proposed to the celebrated Author the problem of finding the most suitable
outline for ships" (Cohen 204).[9] From an examination of the manuscripts, D. T.
Whiteside is inclined to doubt this claim, but suggests that a similar afterthought
a little further on may have been added to the completed manuscript (Newton,
Papers 6:463n).[10] Whatever the exact nature of the change, it seems likely that
Craige was in fact responsible for a very minor alteration in the *Principia.*
At the time of this visit in 1685, Newton was, by his own testimony, already
complaining to Craige about Leibniz's claims to the calculus, although the dispute
did not openly erupt until 1710.[11] A. Rupert Hall's detailed study of the dispute,
however, discusses Craige's early works in the calculus in a rather different light:
"The amazing fact is the very slight allusion to Newton's work, even on the part
of a mathematician who had personally consulted him at Cambridge. . . . Thus
by silent implication, Craige's evidence also testifies to Newton's having no
feelings of criticism toward Leibniz in 1685 or any desire to proclaim to the world
that *he* had been the first to discover a general process of differentiation and
exploit its applications. He left Craige's warm feelings for Leibniz undisturbed"
(Hall 79–80). Although he carried on a dispute with Tschirnhaus on behalf of
Barrow over the next several years, Craige seems to have tried to resist being
drawn into controversy. In his first treatise he carefully adopts a position of
neutrality, employing the Leibnizian notation, acknowledging the work of Leibniz
and Barrow while clearly deferring to the authority of Newton, and raising the
dispute only to distance himself from it: "The thing is not of so much importance
that it seems worthy of any further discussion, especially to me who am neither
English nor Batavian" (*Methodus* 2).[12]

Certainly Craige's warm reception at Cambridge must have encouraged him, and we should view it as a mark of his abilities. In 1687, the same year that Craige took his M.A. at Edinburgh University, James Craige, who had been deprived of the living at Tranent six years earlier for refusing the Sacramental Test, was admitted minister of the Canongate where he succeeded Alexander Burnet, Gilbert Burnet's second cousin. Shortly thereafter, John Craige moved to London, his arrival almost directly coinciding with a more famous one—that of William and Mary. In December of 1688, William of Orange entered the city hours after the departure of James II. Craige was still in Edinburgh on 30 January 1688/89 when he wrote to Colin Campbell. On 13 February, William and Mary were proclaimed King and Queen of England. The following day they were jointly crowned, with Gilbert Burnet, who had served as a close adviser throughout the revolution, officiating as Clerk of the Closet. On 5 March, William recommended Burnet for preferment to the see of Salisbury; on 18 March, a warrant was issued confirming his election; and on 5 April, another warrant was issued granting him temporalities.

Presumably Craige ventured to London that spring seeking preferment. On 29 April, his name first appears in the diary of Robert Hooke, the Gresham College professor and scientist: "J. Craig call'd here" (117). Soon his appearance in Hooke's diary is a daily event, as he met with Edmond Halley and other Fellows of the Royal Society at Jonathan's Coffee House. According to the entry for 13 May, Craige "lyes at the Stirrup in Shoo Lane" (121). His name appears periodically in the diary as he exchanges books and papers with Hooke until 16 July when he makes his last appearance for several years in the cryptic entry: "To Craig: executed 16: porter at Kings armes Holburn bridge" (136). The "Glorious Revolution" that brought William to the throne without bloodshed was followed by a rash of executions (sometimes without trial) designed to crush any lingering Jacobite loyalties; in all likelihood, Hooke's entry refers to attending one of these public executions.

Craige's sudden disappearance from Hooke's diary in July 1689 is probably due to his receiving an appointment as curate. For the rest of his life, Craige's career was in the see of Salisbury. On 24 February 1691/92, he was collated vicar of Potterne; this living (valued in the King's Book at £20 6s. 8d.) was in the peculiar jurisdiction of the bishop. In 1696, he became vicar of Gillingham Major (one of the most prosperous livings in the diocese, valued at £40 17s. 6d.). In addition, he was collated prebend of Durnford (valued at £30) in 1708, and in 1726 he became prebend of Gillingham (valued at £54). His brother, William, collated rector of Upwey (valued at £18 3s.) in 1705, was installed prebend of Gillingham in 1698. When William was collated prebend of Westminster Abbey in 1720, Gilbert Burnet, son of the former bishop, became prebend of Gillingham;

Burnet was in turn succeeded on his death in 1726 by John Craige. One of Craige's acts as prebend of Durnford (1708–26) was to collate his own son, Gilbert, vicar of Durnford in 1723.

Under the direction of Burnet, the leading latitudinarian Whig of his generation, the see of Salisbury became a stronghold of religious toleration and political Whiggery.[13] In such an environment, Craige found a good deal of encouragement for his own religious and political inclinations. Burnet encouraged numerous latitudinarians through appointments to church livings. Thus, as canons of Salisbury Cathedral, John and William Craige enjoyed the company of Francis Fox (a radical Whig latitudinarian who succeeded John Craige as vicar of Potterne in 1708), Peter Allix, William Wotton, John Colbatch, Gilbert Burnet (the bishop's son), and John Hoadly, among others. When Burnet attempted unsuccessfully to replace the current dean of the cathedral with one more sympathetic to his politics, Richard Bentley and Samuel Bradford headed his list of desirable candidates.[14]

Craige's mathematical abilities, combined with his latitudinarian connections, led to his marginal contribution to the conflict between ancients and moderns satirized in Swift's *Battle of the Books* in 1704. In the decade following the Glorious Revolution, two major figures involved on the side of the moderns were William Wotton and Richard Bentley. In 1691, Bentley turned to his friend Wotton for assistance in understanding Newton's *Philosophiae Naturalis Principia Mathematica*. Wotton, in turn, wrote to Craige for advice. Craige's response, dated from Windsor, 21 June 1691, is more often quoted than anything else he ever wrote.[15] The voluminous plan of reading Craige described so intimidated Bentley that he wrote directly to Newton and received from him a much shorter list. In December of that year, the will of Robert Boyle, establishing the famous Boyle Lectures, was probated. Bentley was chosen to deliver the first course of lectures in 1692. For his argument against atheists and deists, he chose to speak on the theological implications of natural philosophy, drawing heavily on Newton's *Principia*. Craige probably attended these lectures, for the subject would certainly have interested him, and it is likely he was spending a great deal of time in the vicinity of the lectures, which were held in the parish of St. Martin-in-the-Fields. On 22 July of the following year, 1693, "The Rev. Mr. John Craige, 30, vicar of Potterne co., Wilts." took out a license to marry "Agnes Cleland, 24, of St. Martin-in-the-Fields" (Chester and Armytage 2:315). They were married in that parish by her father, the Reverend Mr. John Cleland, vicar of Linwood in Lincolnshire, five days later.[16]

Craige must have been combining business with pleasure that summer, for in June 1693 he published *Tractatus Mathematicus de Figurarum Curvilinearum Quadraturis & Locis Geometricis* (*A Mathematical Treatise on the Quadrature and Geometrical Loci of Curvilinear Figures*). In the preface to this treatise, Craige continued to make use of the Leibnizian notation and freely confessed his indebtedness to Leibniz in the following words:

Lest I should seem to ascribe too much to myself or to detract from others, I freely acknowledge that the differential calculus of Leibniz has supplied me with such aid in coming upon these matters, that without it, I had hardly been able to pursue these concerns with the facility that I hoped; with what amount of work our most celebrated author has advanced the cause of solid and advanced geometry with this one most noble discovery cannot be concealed from the most skilled Geometers of the present age, and what its utility has been in finding the dimensions of figures this following tract will sufficiently declare.[17]

Though hardly calculated to curry favor among English mathematicians, Craige's open declaration of indebtedness to Leibniz helped secure his reputation on the continent. Leibniz's own journal, the *Acta Eruditorum,* went so far as to rank Craige among the originators of the calculus—before Newton, though of course after Leibniz.[18]

During the eighteenth century, Craige's reputation prospered on the continent even as it suffered in England, perhaps in part because his early works seem to espouse Leibniz's claims to priority in the Newton-Leibniz controversy. Even the staunchest Leibnizians, however, had difficulty reconciling this early pro-Leibnizian position with Craige's clear support for Newton's claims once the controversy became public (see, for example, Titius on this subject in his preface). It is clear that Newton indicated to Craige his displeasure with Leibniz's claims when he showed him his manuscripts, including *De Analysi,* which demonstrated that though Newton had not published his method, he had been employing it for some time. It is likely that he also then mentioned to Craige the hints that he had sent to Leibniz during an earlier correspondence. With this background, the turning point in Craige's allegiance probably came in 1695 when he began to study closely the works being published in Leibniz's *Acta Eruditorum.* On 11 April, he wrote to David Gregory from Potterne:

I cannot ommitt acquainting you, that for want of other imployment I have been at the pains to examine the mathematical Tracts published in the Acta Eruditorum, more nicely than I had ever done before; & I can make it appear that the greatest part of the most important ones, are nothing but what have been done by others, drest up in a new forme, & so disguised as to make them pass for originals. And this not by obscure hints only, but so plainly that any one may plainly [distinguish it *del.*] perceive it. I could wish heartily that some body would write a sheet or two in vindication of the true Authors, for I look upon this base course, that these forraign mathematicians do take not only as a piece of great injustice, but also as a great hindrance to the promotion of learning; while men of parts are spending that time in disguising the inventions of others, which might be more profitably spent improving their own; If any one would undertake this task, I could furnish them with some considerable materials for the work; I know no man could do it better than J: Arbuthnot if he would be at the pains.

By this time, Craige was establishing himself as an authority on modern developments in mathematics. In July of 1694, William Wotton's *Reflections on Ancient and Modern Learning* appeared. In the growing controversy between "Ancients" and "Moderns," Wotton's book was a major modern text and the specific provocation of Swift's *Battle of the Books*. The book compares ancient and modern learning in various disciplines, invariably to the advantage of the moderns. Wotton enlisted two "Modern" experts in his cause: Edmond Halley wrote the chapter on "Ancient and Modern Astronomy and Opticks" (161–68), and John Craige wrote the chapter on "Ancient and Modern Geometry and Arithmetic" (276–82). Two years later, when Craige wrote the first two chapters of the *Theology* (the last four chapters were presumably written at an earlier date), he enjoyed a small but established reputation as a mathematician.[19]

While John Craige was employing mathematics in solidifying his connections with the moderns, his brother, William, seems to have availed himself of Bishop Burnet's political connections following the Glorious Revolution. In 1696, he was granted a minor, unspecified position in the Royal Household of the Duke of Gloucester, who was then eight years old. This appointment was almost certainly due to the efforts of Gilbert Burnet, who had been appointed tutor and preceptor to the Duke. The position was unfortunately short-lived, for the Duke was a sickly child who succumbed to fever in 1699. Precisely what position William held for the next eight years is uncertain, but when Mary Finch, daughter of the Earl of Nottingham and widow of the Marquis of Halifax, remarried John Ker, first Duke of Roxburgh, William definitely held a position in the new household (*H.M.C. Roxburgh* 53). Ker was keeper of the Privy Seal of Scotland and for a time was Secretary of State. Over the next thirteen years, William served as secretary to the Duke of Roxburgh, underkeeper of the Privy Seal, and tutor to Robert, second Duke of Roxburgh (*H.M.C. Portland* 10:343; Chester 302 n.2). It is probable that the family moved to Westminster, for Mary Finch was buried there in 1718 ("John Ker, first Duke of Roxburgh," *DNB*). If they did move, it is most likely that the family played a role in William's appointment to the prebend of Westminster Abbey in 1720.[20] While the full extent of William's political connections cannot be known with absolute certainty, the men with whom he was aligned following the Glorious Revolution (Marlborough, Burnet, Nottingham, Halifax, and Roxburgh) played a significant role in the formation of the Whig party.

While William Craige was enjoying the patronage of Burnet and Roxburgh, John Craige was taking in mathematics students at his home and receiving the patronage of Gilbert Burnet. William Burnet, the bishop's eldest son and later governor of New York, was sent down from Trinity College, Cambridge, in 1701, and his father sent him to live for a year with Craige. Although it is not clear exactly what the boy's offense was, a letter from father to tutor dated 1 January 1701/2 reveals the degree of paternal indignation excited in the bishop:

I'll send him one triall more and will keep him with Mr. Craig at Gillingham till he has got there Mathematicks and Philosophy. . . . I will send Mr. [William] Craig down to bring him up as I intend to send him down with him to settle him at his brothers for I have now so little pleasure in him that I will not suffer him to be much in my sight. . . .

[p.s.] The date remembers me to wish you a happy new year I can say nothing to the boy but God pity him.

In 1708, Craige was installed prebend of Durnford and canon of Salisbury Cathedral. Three years later, probably with Burnet's endorsement, he was elected a Fellow of the Royal Society. Burnet seems to have been attempting to gain for Craige some more advanced position in the cathedral in early 1714. Sir Richard Howe, Tory M.P. for Wiltshire, wrote from London on 3 March 1713/14 to Robert Harley, Earl of Oxford:

I expect every moment to receive the ill news of the death of a very worthy canon of Salisbury Cathedral, which loss would be in a great degree repaired by the speedy choice of another of eminent character, if the Chapter were permitted to proceed to a free election. But it is no little affliction as well as surprise to me to be informed that some great persons have formed so strong an interest for one Mr. Craig, a Scotchman, and creature of the Bishop of Salisbury, that the Chapter is likely to be strongly influenced in his favour. Mr. Craig is a person looked upon as disaffected to the interest of the Church, and a constant opposer of her Majesty's most loyal subjects. I am sure I speak the sense of all the worthy clergy and gentry of the county of Wilts. (*H.M.C. Portland* 5:388–89)

The letter makes clear that Gilbert Burnet had singled out John Craige for preferment, and the choice prompted strong opposition among the Tories. If Craige had reason to hope for preferment within the church in March 1713/14, those hopes were dealt a severe blow a year later. On 17 March 1714/15, Gilbert Burnet died in his home in St. John's Court in London; he was buried in the nearby parish church of St. James, Clerkenwell. Burnet had moved to London following the death of his third wife in 1710. It was about this time that Craige moved to London in what biographers refer to as a "disappointed" hope "of being noticed for his mathematical abilities" ("John Craig," *DNB*). In 1713, M. Deslandes describes a visit to London in which he dined at the home of Sir Isaac Newton. Rounding out the dinner party were Edmond Halley, Abraham DeMoivre, and John Craige—in Deslande's words, "all mathematicians of the first order" (Brewster 2:257). If Craige was, in fact, hoping for recognition, we must grant him a fair amount of success.

Craige was essentially without a patron following Burnet's death. He seems to have shifted his target and pinned his hopes on political rather than religious patronage. Burnet's kinsman, George Cheyne, had published his *Philosophical Principles of Natural and Revealed Religion* in 1705; in 1715, he brought out a second edition with an added second part containing three chapters on the nature of infinity. The third chapter, "On the Arithmetick of Infinities," was written by Craige. This second edition of the work was dedicated to John, Duke of Roxburgh, in whose household William Craige was employed as a tutor. In 1718, Craige published his final work, *De Calculo Fluentium,* and dedicated it to James Stanhope, who had become Secretary of State during the "Whig Split" of 1717. This shakeup in power, proceeding from the widening rift between George I and his son, resulted in Stanhope occupying the leadership role that had belonged to Sir Robert Walpole in the previous ministry. Where Walpole was a consummate politician who rose to power as a parliamentary leader, Stanhope was very much a King's minister. His fierce loyalty and zealous devotion to his sovereign's interest earned him his monarch's trust and rewards.

If Craige was seeking political patronage, his luck was poor. Only a few months after the publication of *De Calculo Fluentium,* Walpole led the opposition in Parliament to soundly defeat Stanhope's Peerage Bill and drastically limit his influence. Then in 1721, as the economy worsened and the South Sea Bubble Crisis came to a head, Stanhope died suddenly. George reconciled himself to his son and brought Walpole into the ministry as Chancellor of the Exchequer and First Lord of the Treasury. When the South Sea Bubble burst in 1722, effectively discrediting the remainder of Stanhope's ministry, Walpole consolidated his power. Over the next two decades, he was the dominant force in English politics. Craige retired to the quiet life of a country clergyman in Dorset.

That Craige was searching for a source of income at this time can be deduced from references to him in the correspondence of Thomas Burnet and George Duckett. In a letter of 18 March 1717/18, responding to an inquiry by Duckett, Burnet writes:

> I enquired of Craig, whether he continued to teach the Mathematicks and to board young Gentlemen in his house, but without mentioning your having a Kinsman that you would send to him, or anything about you. He answered me that he would be very glad to teach any young Gentleman the Mathematicks, that were lodged in any part of the Country near him; that he should be very unwilling to take in any one as a Boarder, because his Children being all grown up, he should be thereby straightened for Room; that if any of his friends were desirous he should do it, some Children's ages requiring them to be under the inspection of an immediate Master, he was resolved beforeha[nd] to know the age of the Person, and the Terms he should be upon. (Burnet, *Letters* 146–47)

And again on 6 April: "As to the business about John Craig, he told me that he would be very ready to board a Gentleman that was 21 years of age, . . . I enquired of him as to the Price, what he would expect; he told me the same that my Brother or Mr. Speake gave him; what that was I cannot tell" (150). Not only does Craige here indicate a willingness "to teach any young Gentleman the

Mathematicks" as he had Burnet's brother in 1701, but he also confesses else-where in the letter that he has attempted to solve the problem of longitude. The problem enjoyed a certain notoriety, especially among the wits of the day, as the current pointless quest of the new science—a new philosopher's stone. Thus, for instance, Hogarth's fourth plate of "The Rake's Progress," showing the rake in Bedlam, depicts a lunatic in one corner calculating longitudes on the wall of his cell. The heavy dose of skepticism about the project shared by Craige and his friends suggests that his primary motive in attempting the problem was the healthy reward offered by Parliament.

On 5 March 1717/18, Burnet writes to Duckett: "John Craig is in Town, but I believe upon no such Gimcracks as the Longitude; family affairs have brought him to Town, but I believe he has also a Mathematical book to print" (Burnet, *Letters* 144). In the following letter of 18 March, Burnet writes: "As to John Craig's being in Town on the score of the Longitude, he would fain have made a secret of it to me, and deny'd it flatly, till I not only quoted you as having heard it for certain, but Tom Freek to whom he himself had declared it. I find that however sure he thought himself of it, some time ago, he now is very hopeless of success; but Sir Isaac Newton is so far of his opinion, that if ever that great Secret be discovered, it will be by such tables of the Eclipses, as John could not come to an exact calculation of" (146).

In June of 1720, William Craige was installed as prebend of Westminster Abbey. The prebend of Gillingham Major that he vacated was bestowed upon Gilbert Burnet, second son of the bishop, by Bishop Talbot. In the winter of 1720/21, an epidemic of smallpox swept through London. William Craige died on 19 February; he was buried in Westminster Abbey on the twenty-fifth (Chester 302 n. 2).

William's will mentions only three family members: his widow, Mary, who proved the will; his brother, John, who is named residuary legatee and who inherited all his books; and a niece, Agnes, who was John's eldest daughter. The terms of Mary's will, leaving a considerable estate and proved in 1746, yield some additional information. The only beneficiary named Craig in her will is a niece, Magdalen, to whom she bequeaths ten pounds per annum (Chester 368 n. 8). This bequest was revoked by a codicil dated 1744.

For the last ten years of his life after the death of his brother, Craige lived a life of quiet retirement. The only official record we have of him is in 1726. In that year, Gilbert Burnet died at the age of 31, and the prebend of Gillingham Major was given by Bishop Hoadly to Craige, who kept it until his death in 1731. Gillingham Major was the wealthiest living in the deed and gift of the see of Salisbury. Excepting the years 1720–26, when it was given to Gilbert Burnet, it remained in the hands of the Craiges from 1697 to 1731. On 11 October 1731, the Reverend Mr. John Craige of High Holbourne died at the age of 68 or 69.

He was buried three days later in the churchyard of St. James, Clerkenwell, in whose church his longtime friend and patron, Gilbert Burnet, was buried (*Parish Registers* 211). Craige died intestate, and an administration "was issued to William Craig the natural and legitimate son"; in 1746, with the estate still unadministered and William now "also deceased," a new administration was granted to "Magdalen Craig spinster the natural and lawfull daughter of [John Craige]."

3

Mathematical Principles of the *Theology*

JOHN CRAIGE WAS, BEFORE ALL ELSE, A MATHEMATICIAN, AND *THE MATHEmatical Principles of Christian Theology* is principally a mathematical work. In this respect, its two most noteworthy features are its attempt to apply mathematical calculus to the probability of human testimony and its use of the geometric principles of the recently developed calculus of fluents.[1] Early in his preface, Craige attributes to Plato the claim that "God geometrizes" (Appendix 53). Craige was, both by training and inclination, a geometer, and he made no use of what we consider probability theory, a fact that has hurt his reputation with historians. Thus, for Ian Hacking, the *Theology* indicates that Craige "had no conception of probability logic" (*Emergence* 70).

In fact, Craige's avoidance of probability theory should be understood as motivated by a deliberate rejection rather than by ignorance. Craige pursues an essentially geometric model of comparative probabilities that in some ways anticipates the modern statistical notion of a log likelihood ratio. Stephen Stigler, who first proposed this reading of Craige, accepts the view that Craige's mathematical notion of probability is essentially naive, suggesting that he arrived at an approximation of modern logistic regression by bypassing conventional probability because "Craig was effectively operating *de novo*" (5). As we have seen, however, Craige was already recognized as one of the more perceptive and capable mathematicians of his day, and he was certainly acquainted with those works by Halley, DeMoivre, and Arbuthnot that introduced Pascal's probability theory into England. In the chapter "On Ancient and Modern Mathematicks" that he contributed to Wotton's *Reflections on Ancient and Modern Learning* in 1694, Craige makes no mention of probability theory, although as a distinctly modern field it would seem ideally suited to his argument that modern mathematics is superior to that of the ancients. Craige's method can be seen to reveal a mistrust of the inductive method of probability theory as well as a fundamentally different set of assumptions about the meaning of probability.

A formal mathematical theory of probability was first conceived during the summer of 1654 in the correspondence of Blaise Pascal and Pierre Fermat.

Though mathematicians had occasionally dealt with problems in probability before this time, no one had ever formulated a general theory such as that articulated by Pascal and Fermat. The theoretical foundation established that summer was developed extensively by a number of mathematicians in the decade that followed. Pascal had captured the imagination of the mathematical world when he wrote in the *Traité de Triangle Arithmetique:*

> The subject has hitherto dwelt in uncertainty; but after being refractory to experiment, it has now been brought into the domain of reason. I have so surely reduced it to an art by geometry, that, sharing in geometry's certitude, it may boldly develop. And thus, joining mathematical demonstration to the uncertainty of chance, and conciliating what seems to be contrary, it takes its title from both sides, and justly gives itself this astonishing denomination: the geometry of chance.[2] (Trans. qtd. in Bishop 88)

Pascal's description of the "geometry of chance" reflects the metaphysical considerations that prompted his discovery. He hopes to reduce to the "domain of reason" those "outcomes of ambiguous fate" that are "justly attributed to chance contingency" (*Oeuvres* 102). The expressed desire parallels the function of Providence in Christian metaphysics—an ability to discern a rational ordering behind an apparently random fate. The phrase "I have reduced . . . by geometry" (*per geometriam reduximus*) may suggest the nature of the anxiety behind the concern with probability/Providence. For implicit in Pascal's language (which became commonplace in eighteenth-century treatises) is an association of the finite with the "domain of reason" and of the infinite with "ambiguous fate," while mathematics mediates between the two.

Both the anxiety generated by the idea of the infinite and the use of probability as an aid to prudence in moral dilemmas (accurately judging future outcomes in the present on the basis of past performances) are apparent in Pascal's most famous exercise in probability—"the wager." The wager is an argument designed to show that it is in one's self-interest to believe in God (*not* that one should believe out of self-interest). Pascal likens our knowledge of God to our knowledge of infinity. We are aware of the concept of infinity, and at the same time we are ignorant of its nature. Infinity cannot be odd since for every odd number there exists a greater even number; infinity cannot be even since for every even number there exists a greater odd number. He contends in the *Pensées* that our uncertain knowledge of the nature of infinity is analogous to our uncertain knowledge of the nature of God: "At the extremity of this infinite distance a game is in progress, where either heads or tails may turn up. What will you wager?"(Br. 233).[3] As we have no certain knowledge of the outcome, the wise choice is not to wager at all, but life is such that either one believes or one does not believe—you are in the game and you must wager. Having determined that one must choose, the question remains whether it is in the player's best interest to believe or disbelieve in God.

Such a decision is made, Pascal reasons, by consulting one's happiness. One who wagers to believe is risking a finite happiness for the return of the infinite happiness of the kingdom of heaven. Likewise, if one wagers to disbelieve, he is risking an infinite happiness for the finite happiness of the present life. In such a case it is in man's self-interest to believe:

> But what about your happiness? Let us weigh the gain and the loss involved by wagering that God exists. Let us estimate the two cases: if you win, you win all; if you lose, you lose nothing. . . . There is an eternity of life and happiness. . . . There is an infinity of infinitely happy life to win, one chance of winning against a finite number of chances of losing, and what you stake is finite. That removes all doubt as to choice; whatever the infinite is, and there is not an infinity of chances of loss against the chance of winning, there are no two ways about it, all must be given.[4] (Br. 233)

Chapters 3–6 of Craige's *Theology* are mathematical elaborations of a version of this argument. In each case, the argument reveals an anxiety of uncertainty. Pascal's argument culminates at the close of the wager and at the beginning of the thought that follows (at least, according to one editor of the *Pensées*) with a weighing of the certain finite against the uncertain infinite. This is the moral application of probability:

> For it is no use alleging the uncertainty of winning and the certainty of risk, or to say that the infinite distance between the certainty of what one risks and the uncertainty of what one will win equals that between the finite good, which one certainly risks, and the infinite, which is uncertain. That is not so; every player risks a certainty to win an uncertainty, and yet he risks a finite certainty to win a finite uncertainty, without offending reason. There is no infinite distance between the certainty risked and the uncertainty of the gain; that is false. There is, indeed, infinity between the certainty of winning and the certainty of losing, but the uncertainty of winning is proportionate to the certainty of what is risked, according to the proportion of chances of gain and loss. Hence, if there are as many risks on one side as on the other, the right course is to play even; and then the certainty of the risk is equal to the uncertainty of the gain, so far are they from being infinitely distant. Thus our proposition is of infinite force, when there is the infinite at stake in a game where there are equal chances of winning and losing, but the infinite to win. This is conclusive, and if men are capable of truth at all, there it is.
>
> If a man should do nothing except on the strength of what is certain, he ought to do nothing on that of religion, for it is not certain. Yet how many things he does on the strength of what is uncertain—sea voyages, battles! I say then that nothing at all should be done, for nothing is certain, and that there is more certainty in religion than there is as to whether we shall see tomorrow; for it is not certain that we shall see tomorrow, but it is certainly possible that we may not see it. One cannot say as much about religion. It is not certain that it is true, but who will venture to say that

it is certainly possible that it is not? Now, when one works for tomorrow, and for an uncertainty, he acts with reason, because according to the doctrine of chances already demonstrated, one ought to work for the uncertain.[5] (Br. 233, 234)

The anxiety of certitude and the palliative offered by probability are clearly expressed in these two passages. The competition between "the finite good, which one certainly risks" and "the infinite, which is uncertain" manifests itself in the very language of the passage as the various cognates of the key terms pursue one another, leading to a reliance on "the doctrine of chances." For Pascal and the early developers of probability who followed him, probability theory offered a tool as well suited to moral as to mathematical calculations by offering a rational rule or guide that parallelled the function of prudence in Christian metaphysics.

Early practitioners followed Pascal in attempting to show that the "uncertainties of chance" obeyed mathematical laws. Thus, Dr. John Arbuthnot published in 1692 *Of the Laws of Chance,* and Abraham DeMoivre writes in 1712 *The Doctrine of Chances.* In his preface, DeMoivre writes, "We may imagine Chance and Design to be, as it were, in competition with each other, for the production of some sorts of Events, and may calculate what Probability there is, that those Events should be rather owing to one than to the other" (v–vi). In dedicating this work to Sir Isaac Newton, DeMoivre writes:

> I should think my self very happy, if having given my Readers a Method of calculating the Effects of Chance, as they are the result of Play, and thereby fixing certain Rules, for estimating how far some sort of Events may rather be owing to Design than Chance, I could by this small Essay excite in others a desire of prosecuting these studies, and of learning from your Philosophy how to collect, by a just Calculation, the Evidences of exquisite Wisdom and Design, which appear in the *Phenomena* of Nature throughout the Universe.

Craige's *Theology* is written from within this metaphysical tradition, and while its aims are undeniably bizarre, they are substantially no different from those of other respected, even celebrated, works. A closer look at Craige's use of the concept of probability reveals both what was acceptable as metaphysical applications of mathematics and what it was in Craige's work that touched off such a violent response.

Although the treatise has most often been discussed as an early contribution (of dubious value) to the emerging field of probability theory, Craige was in fact working out of a background in the geometrical foundations of the equally new field of the calculus of fluents. In the history of the fluxional calculus, he has earned a small but established reputation. He was one of the very first in England to comprehend the power of the new mathematics, and his publications and contributions to the *Philosophical Transactions of the Royal Society* made him a leader in developing the calculus. David Gregory's notebooks reveal that he sometimes referred to a species of curve as a Craigean curve after Craige's method of determining the area described by it. Craige's first work in 1685 was the earliest to use the now standard Leibnizian notation of dx and dy in place of the Newtonian dot notation in England, and his second work in 1693 was the first to introduce the Leibnizian symbol of integration, $\int$. Raphson's *History of Fluxions* (largely prompted by Newton in an attempt to discredit Leibniz's claims of priority) makes much of the contributions of Craige, devoting an entire chapter to reprinting his "method of squaring irrational curves" (51–60). The Leibnizians, as well as the Newtonians, were willing for other reasons to subscribe to this same version of history, and Newton complained of the editors of *Acta Eruditorum* "[who] everywhere insinuate to their readers that ye method of fluxions is the differential method of Mr Leibnitz & in such a manner as if he was the true author & I had taken it from him, & give such an account of the Booke of Quadratures as if it was nothing else then an improvement of what had been found out before by Mr Leibnitz Dr Sheen [Cheyne] & Mr Craig" (Newton, *Correspondence* 5:117).[6]

For the most part, Craige's mathematical argument in the *Theology* relies on the foundations laid by the geometrical investigations of motion conducted by Leibniz, Newton, and Isaac Barrow. Craige tried to remain outside the quarrel over priority; he drew freely from both Leibniz and Newton, and if he used the notation of one, he frequently bolstered his arguments with references to Newton's large body of unpublished work. Throughout his writings, however, it is clear how deeply he was influenced by Barrow's *Geometrical Lectures*. Craige's first work had included an attack on Tschirnhaus for plagiarizing from the works of Leibniz and Barrow. When Leibniz came to Tschirnhaus's defense, asserting that he did not feel victimized, Craige responded by annexing to his next work a detailed account of the plagiarism from Barrow, which Raphson subsequently took note of, "as Mr. Craig justly complains" (1). If in part this indicates the degree to which Craige, however unwillingly, was being drawn at least to the periphery of the Leibniz-Newton quarrel, it also reveals something of his regard for Barrow's contribution.

The absence of probability theory in Craige's treatise is underlined when we compare it with the response to it published anonymously by George Hooper in *Philosophical Transactions*. Hooper had published an earlier, nonmathematical version of this argument in a sermon in 1689, but there can be little doubt that he presented this new formulation with its reliance on probability theory in reply to Craige. In the first two chapters of the *Theology*, Craige seeks to quantify the rate at which a history loses its credibility. Chapter 1, "Concerning Historical Probability Transmitted Orally," develops the notion that the original probability of an account is affected adversely by three factors: the number of retellings, distance, and the passage of time. His second chapter, concerning written transmission, follows this same model while noting that written histories enjoy greater original probability than oral histories, suspicion regarding errors of transcription arise more slowly than those regarding errors of retelling, and written texts enjoy a longer life than oral accounts. In each chapter he focuses on the history of Jesus Christ as an example, determining that insofar as that history depends on oral tradition, its probability disappeared about A.D. 800, but that the probability of the written account in the Gospel would not disappear before A.D. 3150.

Although Hooper refrains from making explicit the application of his argument to Craige's problem concerning the credibility of the Gospel, his essay seems calculated to refute Craige's conclusions. Thus, he follows Craige in considering the credibility of successive and then of concurrent narrators and the credibility of oral and of written testimony. Where Craige's hypothesis that the life of a written text was two hundred years led him to the conclusion that it would take 3150 years for the probability of the written history of Christ to disappear (Appendix 70), Hooper's assumption that the life of a singly written text was restricted to "the space of a 100, if not 200 years" led him to conclude "that written Tradition, if preserved but by a single Succession of Copies, will not lose half of its full Certainty [and so become subject to disbelief] until Seventy times a Hundred (if not Two Hundred) Years are Past" ("A Calculation" 364). Hooper arrives at his figures by an attempt to quantify the probability of an account according to the methods of Huygenian expectations. If an account originally had a degree of probability equal to $a/(a+c)$, then after n successive narrations, its probability is $[a/(a+c)]^n$. Craige's argument, on the other hand, makes no attempt to measure the probability of the account itself, but only the rate at which the original probability is diminished by suspicions arising from retelling, distance, and the passage of time. Thus, while Hooper's formulation looks familiar, Craige's probability is expressed by the unusual formula:

$$P = x + (m - 1)s + T^2k/t^2 + D^2q/d^2 \text{ (Appendix 61)}$$

In this equation, P represents the probability currently enjoyed by a text, x represents its original probability, and s, k, and q represent the suspicions of this account generated by the number of retellings, the passage of time, and the elapsed distance, respectively. The number of witnesses through whom an account is successively transmitted is represented by m, and T and D represent time and distance in units of measurement t and d.

Only recently has Craige's idiosyncratic formulation been remarked upon when Stephen Stigler proposed that Craige's "probability" should be understood not in its customary sense, but rather as an extraordinarily early anticipation of our notion of a "log likelihood ratio" (5–7). Stigler's proposal is attractive in that it makes sense of an otherwise erratic formulation, and it provides a meaningful basis for grasping Craige's argument.

Stigler's suggestion has been anticipated in a more general sense by C. S. Peirce in a way that seems more useful to understanding the historical issues at work. Drawing on terminology used by J. A. Venn, Peirce distinguishes the "materialist" view of probability, which has to do with the frequency of occurrence, from the "conceptualist" view of probability, which has to do with the feeling of belief that ought to be attached to a proposition (291). Hacking has argued that the emergence of probability theory around 1660 depended on the conjunction of these two views in an appreciation of probability's "duality" (*Emergence* 11–18). However true that may be on the grand scale, Craige's view of probability in 1699 is clearly conceptualist. After noting that feelings of belief should correlate to observed likelihood, Peirce proposes the log likelihood ratio as the appropriate means of measuring conceptualist probability in language tailored to an argument such as Craige's:

> As the chance diminishes the feeling of believing should diminish, until an even chance is reached, where it should completely vanish and not incline either toward or away from the proposition. When the chance becomes less, then a contrary belief should spring up and should increase in intensity as the chance diminishes, and as the chance almost vanishes (which it can never quite do) the contrary belief should tend toward an infinite intensity. Now there is one quantity which, more simply than any other, fulfills these conditions; it is the logarithm of the chance. (294)

As Stigler makes clear, the issue is not whether Craige indicated any "awareness of the complicated mathematical relationship we associate with the term 'log likelihood ratio'," but rather that his formula "may legitimately be viewed as a precursor to modern logistic regression" (2, 7). Understanding Craige's conceptualist view of probability is illuminating in regard to his relation to other contemporary probability arguments. In particular, this proposal meshes with the idea that Craige was not interested in establishing "a measure of uncertainty on a scale of zero to one," but rather that "he was definitely after a concept referring to *changes* in the weight of evidence due to data" (5, 7). Craige is at pains to avoid attaching values to the probability of a text at any given point. While Hooper is thrown back on assuming an arbitrary value for the probability of his narratives ("Let the Reports have, each of them Five Sixths of Certainty" ["A Calculation" 360]), Craige leaves this measurement as an undetermined x and focuses instead on those attendant suspicions that accompany it.[7] His approximation of the log likelihood ratio enables him to compare probabilities and arrive at a relative rather than an absolute measurement: "The present probability of the [written] history of Christ is what one would have who, in the times of Christ himself, had received the same history orally from twenty-eight disciples of Christ" (Appendix 69).

Hooper's work attempts to quantify the probability of a text; his method presupposes that a work possesses a quantifiable degree of probability as an attribute. Craige attempts to measure the change in the reception of a work; his method sets aside any concern with the innate probability of a text to attend to the external factors affecting the reception of the work. They are in fact proceeding from two distinct notions of probability as well as two different sets of assumptions concerning mathematical demonstration. Hooper's measurement concerns the probability inherent in a text; Craige is interested in measuring the degree to which an audience will believe a text.

This marks one way in which the *Theology* is distinct from Craige's other works. Those works directed to an audience of mathematicians develop rigorous mathematical arguments for narrowly defined ends. Here, however, geometric demonstrations serve as rhetorical devices in the service of a philosophical argument (so that J. F. Scott omits any notice of the work in his sketch of Craige's career in the *Dictionary of Scientific Biography*). Thus, Craige writes, for instance, of his third axiom, "This axiom is not to be understood in a mathematically rigorous way" (Appendix 55). In fact, the argument of the first two chapters, which has overshadowed the rest of the treatise, is primarily intended to serve as a necessary step for establishing that "the true Christian is the wisest of all wise men [and] that atheists and deists are the most foolish of all foolish men" (Appendix 83). In this larger sense, Craige should be seen as pursuing Locke's hint that "Morality is Capable of Demonstration, as well as Mathematicks" (*Essay* 516).

In chapters 3–6, Craige borrows the conceptual framework of Pascal's wager to demonstrate that it is rational and wise to believe in God, though in fact (as we shall see below) Craige's immediate source is John Locke's slightly altered version of the wager. For the most part, discussion of the *Theology* ignores these chapters, and it seems safe to say that if his critics read Craige's adaptation of the wager, they accepted it—as Montmort did—as "laudable and pious." Pope, who included Craige in his *Dunciad* because of the *Theology,* also echoed the wager in *An Essay on Man:* "The joy unequal'd, if its end it gain/And if it lose, attended with no pain" (3:4.315–16).

Craige's inclusion in the *Dunciad* and the other attacks on the *Theology* result from his argument in the first two chapters. Craige's argument is only geometric; he does not use the calculus of probabilities to determine likelihood, but instead proposes and applies a hypothetical function for the decay of belief. As Stigler notes, his interest is in change rather than likelihood; his demonstration rests on the geometric foundations of mechanics laid down by Wallis, Barrow, Leibniz, and Newton. It was not on the basis of his mathematics, however, that Craige was attacked. Rather, it was the basic premise of his argument that drew the heavy criticism.

Those who dispute with Craige fall into two groups: those who discuss his argument for the decay of credibility generally, and those who take exception to his theological applications. John Edwards' attack in 1714 is representative of the latter group. Edwards first claims that Craige "undertakes to prove that there is only a Probability of the Truth of the Christian Religion," and then contends, "that his Assertion is groundless and false; for . . . it is plain that the Degrees of Probability of our Saviour's History will not be lessen'd, but increas'd and strengthen'd" (85, 86).

This criticism is borrowed from Humphrey Ditton's more general response to Craige in 1712, which established the foundations on which all subsequent responses were to build (see below). That foundation, however, itself rests on a distortion, for Craige never claimed "that there is only a Probability of the Truth of the Christian Religion." Rather, he claimed that the degree of belief enjoyed by any given historical text, such as the Gospel, changes as a function of time, distance, and retelling. It should not be surprising that Craige was misunderstood on this point, for his argument was novel and his mathematical argument ultimately unpersuasive. It was not until 1755, when Richard Price transmitted Thomas Bayes' letter on decision theory to the Royal Society, that there existed a plausible calculus for determining retrospective probabilities. Bayes' calculus of retrospective probabilities, designed to determine the probability of a historical hypothesis (H) given the evidence of existing testimony (E), provides a mathematical expression for what Hume termed the problem of induction—"the search for some rationally comprehensible connection between past events and future contingencies, or more generally between evidence and hypothesis" (Palter 246). Ultimately, Craige's computations should be seen as anticipating Hume's problem of induction by limiting his use of inductive reasoning to what Peirce would later term abduction or retroduction.

The crux of Ditton's argument appears in proposition 15, where he asserts that "no Testimony is really, and in the Nature of things, rendered less credible by any other Cause, than the loss or want of some of those Conditions which first made it (rationally) credible in such or such a Degree" (137). Ditton's criticism, which formed the basis for the remarks against Craige by Houtteville, Hume, and Pope, confuses belief in a historical account of an event with belief in the event itself. We are to believe an event as it is reported to us unless we receive additional information that contradicts the report or undermines the credibility of the reporter. It is then further argued that if additional information does not dispute, but reaffirms, the original testimony, the reported event becomes even more probable.

This is an argument Craige foresaw and attempted to forestall in his preface to the *Theology* where he distinguishes between the credibility of the events of Christ's life and the credibility of the historical account of these events presented in the Gospel:

I anticipate only two objections of any substance. The first is that I fail to define accurately the time at which the probability of the history of Christ ought to be disappearing, because I take this probability as always decreasing at a certain regular rate, without considering that new degrees of probability will arise from the fulfillment of certain prophecies. But the answer is easy: I have only considered this history of Christ the saviour as it has been transmitted up to this point through so many centuries.[8] (Appendix 54)

Thus, Craige's argument was never (as it was sometimes represented) that over time Christ's existence would become less likely, but rather that over time the degree to which people would believe in the Gospel as historically accurate would lessen. In this light, he appears not only eminently sane, but borne out by subsequent history.

Craige's attempt to establish a continuous function that measures changes in credibility is the most far-reaching example of his indebtedness to Newton and the Newtonian calculus. For the Newtonian calculus of fluxions, or fluents, as distinguished from the Leibnizian calculus of integration proceeds by determining the "moment" of change or flux at every point on a curve: "Newton regarded the curve $f(x,y) = 0$ as the locus of intersection of two moving lines, one vertical and the other horizontal" (C. H. Edwards 191). In a fundamental tract written in 1671, known as the "Tractatus De Methodis Serierum et Fluxionem" (unpublished until a translation appeared in 1736), Newton developed his vocabulary of quantities as fluents whose fluxion refers to the instantaneous speed of flow at any given moment. This is the basic vocabulary of the calculus that Newton refined and used over the next forty years:

I consider time as flowing or increasing by continual flux & other quantities as increasing continually in time & from ye fluxion of time I give the name of fluxions to the velocitys wth wch all other quantities increase. Also from the moments of time I give the name of moments to the parts of any other quantities generated in moments of time. . . . And I found the method not upon summs & differences, but upon the solution of this probleme: *By knowing the Quantities generated in time to find their fluxions.* . . . This Method is derived immediately from Nature her self, that of indivisibles, Leibnitian differences or infinitely small quantities not so. (*Papers* 3:17–18)

From wherever Newton's method derived, his terminology came from Isaac Barrow's opening lecture in *Geometrical Lectures,* as D. T. Whiteside and J. E. Hofmann have already argued (cf. Newton, *Papers* 3:70–72). In following Barrow, Newton writes, "I consider quantities as though they were generated by continuous increase in the manner of a space which a moving object describes in its course" (*Papers* 3:17). This vocabulary that allows one to talk about quantity in terms of the relationship of time, space, and motion—and vice versa—is crucial to Newton's subsequent development of the stabilizing laws of motion, but it also leads to Craige's formulations throughout the final chapters of the *Theology,* in which he relates the quantities of pleasures, according to their intensities and durations.

The emotional responses to Craige's mechanistic argument in the *Theology* may in part be caused by his use of the idea of decay.[9] He was repeatedly misread as predicting the Apocalypse when he claimed only to be setting a limit for the earliest conceivable date. In disputing this distortion, his critics often argued (rather illogically) that events become more credible as time passes. Thus, while Craige's mathematical argument may have been based on sound Newtonian principles and consistent with Newton's own views that barring divine intervention final cosmological decay would result from his account of the nature of matter, Craige's language appeared to subvert the optimistic claims of those Newtonians who read in Newton an argument against decay.[10]

There remains, however, a fundamental methodological distinction between Pascal's calculus of probabilities and Newton's calculus of fluents. The Newtonian calculus of fluents, like Newtonian natural philosophy, offers a more cautious use of induction than does the calculus of probabilities. His carefully induced first principles (conformable with experimental observation) enable one to deduce certain conclusions: given certain conditions, the area under a curve can be determined. Problems in probability rely on a looser notion of induction in that they do not predict certain outcomes, but trends, tendencies, and likelihoods. The statement that "the probability of a coin landing 'heads' equals one-half" offers little predictive utility—and consequently, little opportunity for verification—for any given flip of a coin. Certainly, the coin cannot land "half heads"; we know only that it as likely to land heads as not. Similarly, the statement does not mean that if you flip a coin twice, it will land heads once, but rather that the more often you flip a coin the more closely the occurrence of heads relative to flips will approach one-half.

Craige's choice of the Newtonian calculus of fluents rather than the calculus of probabilities as the vehicle for his argument suggests that he wished to avoid the skeptical problem of induction that probability logic courts. To understand his choice, it may be useful to follow Hacking in using a distinction between modes of inductive reasoning drawn by C. S. Peirce. Peirce distinguishes "inference or decision under uncertainty," which he terms *induction,* from the generation of abstract theory to explain phenomena, which he terms *abduction* or *retroduction* (Hacking, *Emergence* 75). Thus, induction refers to the reasoning employed in probability logic and critiqued by Hume; abduction describes the process commonly known as Baconian or empirical induction. Bacon himself had no use for induction, rejecting it as "puerile" in section 105 of the *Novum Organum* (qtd. in Hacking, *Emergence* 76). The Newtonian method belongs to the Baconian tradition of abduction. Newton's own statements of method, both in *regulae philosophandi* and in the *Opticks,* indicate that while he sees induction as necessary, it must be always subject to empirical confirmation and preparatory to deductive demonstration in mathematics as well as natural philosophy:

> In experimental philosophy we are to look upon propositions collected by general induction from phenomena as accurately or very nearly true, notwithstanding any contrary hypotheses that may be imagined, till such time as other phenomena occur, by which they may either be made more accurate, or liable to exceptions.[11] (*Philosophiae* 2:555)

> As in Mathematicks, so in Natural Philosophy, the Investigation of difficult Things by the Method of Analysis, ought ever to precede the Method of Composition. (*Opticks* 404, Qu. 31)

Newton suggests a willingness to withdraw or modify any induced principle contradicted by experiment, but barring such a contradiction of principles, he claims for the Newtonian method all the certainty of geometric demonstration.

In the *Theology,* Craige makes use of the new analytic geometry to address problems of uncertainty. In chapters 1 and 2 (on the credibility of the Gospel), he closely follows a Newtonian model of change and quantifies belief in the Gospel as a function of time and distance whose rate of change can be determined. In chapters 3–6 (on finite and infinite pleasure), although the idea of the argument is borrowed from Pascal's wager, the mathematical argument is clearly based on Isaac Barrow's *Geometrical Lectures* (the figures Craige uses in his argument may be found in Barrow's opening lecture on simple motion; see especially 21–26). Overshadowing all else, however, is Craige's use of the Newtonian vocabulary that prompted Lubbock and Drinkwater to term the work "an insane parody." *Motion, time, space, force, duration, velocity, intensity, magnitude, uniform, quantity,* and *moment* are all used in a Newtonian sense. Implicit in Craige's argument is the assumption that one can talk about the uncertainties within the mind (such as pleasure and belief) in those same terms that had been successfully applied to the uncertainties of the universe.

Certainly this seems to be the overwhelming weakness of Craige's treatise. One may speak of "the force of an argument" or "being moved to doubt" without fear of being interpreted literally, and yet at the time such a use of Newtonian rhetoric was common—indeed almost necessary. Newton himself tacitly encouraged followers like Craige who attempted to translate arguments from natural philosophy to moral philosophy: "And if Natural Philosophy in all its Parts, by pursuing this Method, shall at length be perfected, the Bounds of Moral Philosophy will be also enlarged" (*Opticks* 405). Craige's attempts to discuss the uncertainties of the mind in terms that had been used profitably in discussing the uncertainty of the universe may appear less ridiculous when set next to the words of David Hume: "For to me it seems evident, that the essence of the mind being equally unknown to us with that of external bodies, it must be equally impossible to form any notion of its powers and qualities otherwise than from careful and exact experiments, and the observation of those particular effects, which result from its different circumstances and situations" (xvii).

If I have placed consideration of an apparently trivial work side by side with what are indisputably some of the greatest developments in the history of mathematics, it is neither to elevate the importance of one nor to denigrate the importance of the others. Rather, my hope has been that in setting these works together we can better discern the ideas and concerns they share as representatives of their age. In the rise of probability and the development of the calculus, we see a concern with the relationship of certainty and uncertainty, the finite and the infinite, and the need for inductive reasoning to extend the bounds of purely deductive demonstrations. If Pascal, speaking of uncertainty, claimed that he had "so surely reduced it to an art by geometry" that it might be "brought into the domain of Reason," then Newton conversely hoped that through his more skeptical use of abduction, "the Bounds of Moral Philosophy will be also enlarged."

4

Intellectual Context of the *Theology*

IF THE MATHEMATICAL FRAMEWORK OF THE *THEOLOGY* DREW UPON THE calculus developed by Newton, then its epistemological framework was provided by Newton and Locke. Craige's debt to Newton went beyond the mathematics and terminology of the *Theology* to include his mechanistic framework and (perhaps) encouragement to attempt applying mathematical arguments to theological issues.[1] Craige probably read Newton's letters to Locke in 1690 detailing "an historical account of two notable corruptions of scripture" (*Correspondence* 2:83). After Newton's death in 1727, his nephew, John Conduitt, began collecting memoirs of his life, to which Craige contributed one that dealt almost exclusively with Newton's theological interests:

> His great application in his inquiries into nature did not make him unmindful of the Great Author of nature. They were little acquainted with him who imagine that he was so intent upon his studies of geometry and philosophy as to neglect that of religion and other things subservient to it. And this I know, that he was much more solicitous in his inquiries into religion than into Natural Philosophy, and that the reason of his shewing the errors of Cartes' philosophy was, because he thought it was made on purpose to be the foundation of infidelity. (Keynes ms. 132)

In this same vein, Newton's correspondence with Richard Bentley concerning the latter's Boyle lectures indicates his willingness to encourage theological applications of his argument set forth in the *Principia*. When Bentley sought his advice on several points concerning revisions in the sermons, Newton began his reply, dated 10 December 1692, by encouraging the project: "When I wrote my treatise about our Systeme I had an eye upon such Principles as might work wth considering men for the beliefe of a Deity & nothing can rejoyce me more then to find it usefull for that purpose" (*Correspondence* 3:233).

Craige's debt to Locke is as profound as his debt to Newton. Every one of Craige's opening definitions in the *Theology* may be traced directly to either Locke or to a synthesis of Locke and Newton. His first axiom, that "every man strives to produce pleasure in his mind, to increase or to persevere in his state of pleasure" (Appendix 55), parallels Locke's discussion of happiness in Book 2 of *An Essay Concerning Human Understanding*.[2] An object, according to Locke, is called Good or Evil "for no other reason, but for its aptness to produce Pleasure and Pain in us, wherein consists our Happiness and Misery. . . . Happiness, under this view, every one constantly pursues, and desires what makes any part of it" (2.21.259; cf. Appendix 71). Moreover, the final four chapters of the *Theology*, concerning pleasure and pain, though ultimately derived from Pascal's *pari*, owe a more immediate debt to Locke's restatement of this argument:

> He that will not be so far a rational Creature, as to reflect seriously upon infinite Happiness and Misery, must needs condemn himself, as not making that use of his Understanding he should. The Rewards and Punishments of another Life, which the Almighty has established, as the Enforcements of his Law, are of weight enough to determine the Choice against whatever Pleasure or Pain this Life can shew, when the eternal State is considered but in its bare possibility, which no Body can make any doubt of. He that will allow exquisite and endless Happiness to be but the possible consequences of a good Life here, and the contrary state the possible Reward of a bad one, must own himself to judge very much amiss, if he does not conclude, That a vertuous Life, with the certain expectation of everlasting Bliss, is to be preferred to a vicious one, with the fear of that dreadful state of Misery . . . when infinite Happiness is put in one scale, against infinite Misery in the other . . . Who can without Madness run the venture? . . . Must it not be a most manifest wrong Judgment that does not presently see, to which side, in this case, the preference is to be given? I have foreborn to mention any thing of the certainty or probability of a future state, designing here to shew the wrong Judgment, that any one must allow, he makes upon his own Principles laid how he pleases, who prefers the short pleasures of a vicious Life upon any consideration, whilst he knows, and cannot but be certain, that a future Life is at least possible. (2.21.281–82)

There are three indications that Locke, and not Pascal, is Craige's immediate source. The emphasis on right and wrong judgment implicit in Pascal's argument becomes the principal focus for both Locke and Craige. In his second and third axioms, Craige defines wisdom as judging according to the value of one's expectations and folly as judging contrary to those values; he concludes that a Christian is the wisest of all wise men and an atheist is the most foolish of fools. He also follows Locke in comparing quantities rather than probabilities. Pascal had concluded that a prudent judgment concerning belief should be made according to the "doctrine of chances," but both Locke and Craige set aside entirely any question of the "probability of a future state," arguing that the barest possibility of such a state decides the issue because of the enormous differences in expectation. This leads to the third indication of Craige's debt to Locke: where Pascal approaches the problem by emphasizing the comparison of certain and uncertain, Locke and Craige emphasize the comparison of finite and infinite. All of these distinctions are part of an overriding distinction of method between Pascal's inductive approach and the Newtonian approach that strives for certain demonstration. Thus, Locke insists on the validity of his argument based on the necessarily induced principle "that a future Life is at least possible."

Just as Craige's chapters concerning pleasure are inspired by Locke's presentation of Pascal's wager, so too, is his attempt to apply mathematical demonstration to that which Locke termed in the *Essay,* "Morality established upon its true foundations" (2.21.281). Locke was immensely respectful of the argumentative power of mathematical demonstration, and he considered it a tool that could and should be turned to questions of morality. On several occasions in the *Essay* (3.11; 4.3; 4.4; 4.12, twice), he presents the argument that "Morality is Capable of Demonstration, as well as Mathematicks" (3.11.516), and he further contends "that moral Knowledge is as capable of real Certainty, as Mathematicks" (4.4.565).

If chapters 3–6 of the *Theology* attempt to apply mathematical demonstration to the moral argument presented in Locke's *Essay,* the moral argument in chapters 1 and 2 is no less influenced by Locke. Craige's hypothesis concerning credibility is clearly derived from Locke's assertion of the natural right of equality in his *Second Treatise on Government.* Craige hypothesizes that "all men have an equal right to be believed unless the contrary has been somehow established. The justice of this hypothesis is founded on this: that all things of the same nature are endowed with the same natural qualities, whether of mind or body, and it is the common practice of mankind, in any business transacted in this life, to accept any man as a witness unless he has somehow lost this natural right" (Appendix 56).[3]

The chain of reasoning that ensues from this hypothesis culminates in Proposition 18, Problem 11: "To define the space of time in which the probability of a written history of Christ will disappear" (Appendix 69).[4] In this problem and throughout the *Theology,* Craige intends by "the probability of a . . . history of Christ" that which Locke, in *The Reasonableness of Christianity,* termed "an historical faith":

> It will be objected by some, that to believe only that Jesus of Nazareth is the Messiah, is but an historical, and not a justifying, or saving faith.
>   To which I answer, That I allow to the makers of systems and their followers to invent and use what distinctions they please, and to call things by what names they think fit. But I cannot allow to them, or to any man, an authority to make a religion for me, or to alter that which God hath revealed. And if they please to call the believing that which our Saviour and his apostles preached, and proposed alone to be believed, an historical faith; they have their liberty. But they must have a care, how they deny it to be a justifying or saving faith, when our Saviour and his apostles have declared it so to be. (101–2)

Locke continues to elaborate on the idea that such a faith in the only essential doctrine proposed in the Gospels. This notion of "an historical faith" was attacked by John Edwards and became the central issue in the controversy surrounding *The Reasonableness of Christianity*. When Craige adopted the notion in the *Theology*, he was entering the lists on the side of Locke and, not surprisingly, drew an attack from the High Church Edwards. More surprising are the responses of those who espoused a rational Christianity but disputed Craige's ideas about probability. Here again, Craige was indebted to Locke. For Craige, probability is defined not mathematically but as probable knowledge:

> 6. Probability is the appearance of agreement, or disagreement, of two ideas, through arguments, whose connexion is not constant, or at least is not perceived to be so.
> 7. Natural Probability is that which is deduced from arguments conformable to our own observation or experience.
> 8. Historical Probability is that deduced from the testimony of others who confirm their own observation or experience.[5] (Appendix 55)

Locke writes in the *Essay:*

> Probability is nothing but the appearance of such an Agreement, or Disagreement [of two Ideas], by the intervention of Proofs, whose connexion is not constant and immutable, or at least is not perceived to be so. . . . The grounds of it are, in short, these two following:
> First, the conformity of any thing with our own Knowledge, Observation, and Experience.
> Secondly, the Testimony of others, vouching their Observation and Experience. (4.15.654, 656)

Although this epistemological definition differs from the mathematical one put forth by Pascal, it exhibits one important similarity: both speak of using reason to reveal hidden connections. Pascal's mathematical definition is a special case of Locke's more general definition. What is important to this new notion of probability is the idea that it is "the domain of reason," whether by "mathematical demonstration" or "the intervention of Proofs," to mediate between two ideas which appear unconnected. Earlier notions of probability had relied not on reason but on being "approved by authority" (Hacking, *Emergence* 30).[6] For Locke, belief is a necessary adjunct to certain knowledge. As certain knowledge must, by its nature, be limited, belief constitutes the greater part of human understanding:

> The entertainment the mind gives this sort of propositions [probable truths] is called *belief, assent,* or *opinion,* which is the admitting or receiving any proposition for true, upon arguments or proofs that are found to persuade us to receive it as true, without certain knowledge that it is so. And herein lies the difference between *probability* and *certainty, faith* and *knowledge;* that in all the parts of knowledge there is intuition; each immediate idea, each step has its visible and certain connexion: in belief, not so. (*Essay* 4.15.655)

So, too, Craige: "For faith is nothing other than that persuasion of the mind, derived from an indeterminate probability, by which we believe certain propositions to be true. If the persuasion arises from certainty, then it is not faith that is being produced, but knowledge. Probability generates faith, but destroys knowledge; certainty, on the other hand, generates knowledge and destroys faith" (Appendix 54).[7]

Unlike certain knowledge, which is absolute, belief or assent is a matter of degree. The need to evaluate these degrees of belief poses a fundamental problem concerning the role of skepticism in human understanding: we need continually to evaluate beliefs, not only of others, but of ourselves as well. "The necessity of believing," writes Locke in the *Essay*, "without Knowledge, nay often upon very slight grounds, in this fleeting state of Action and Blindness we are in, should make us more busy and careful to inform our selves, than constrain others. At least those, who have not thoroughly examined to the bottom all their own Tenets, must confess, they are unfit to prescribe to others; and are unreasonable in imposing that as a Truth on other Men's Belief, which they themselves have not searched into, nor weighed the Arguments of Probability, on which they should receive or reject it" (4.16.660). In his preface to the *Theology*, Craige bases a defense of his argument on this passage: "Those who accept completely all the dogmas of religion will doubtless think that I am undertaking something unsuitable to Christianity in trying to demonstrate its probability. To these I say only that, being preoccupied with their prejudices, they have not yet examined carefully enough the foundations of the religion that they profess; and that they do not rightly understand the nature of faith, which is so much praised in Holy Scripture" (Appendix 53–54).[8]

In response to this need for an evaluation of belief of propositions, Locke classifies all propositions as either subject to observation and experience and therefore "capable of human testimony" or "not capable of human testimony" because they are beyond the senses. Of the first class, termed "matter of fact," Locke gives four arguments for belief and their corresponding degrees of assent. The first of these, which enjoys the greatest degree of belief, is that which concurs with the testimony of all men at all times. Such a belief, called assurance, tells us that the sun will rise tomorrow. Confidence, the second degree of belief, is when one finds by personal observation and the agreement of testimony that "a thing is for the most part so." When there is nothing in the nature of a proposition that speaks favorably or unfavorably as to its truth and it is supported by fair testimony, then belief is "unavoidable." Finally, Locke considers those propositions where testimonies contradict either themselves or common experience. The entertainment the mind gives such propositions, depending on the relative value of the arguments pro and con, is variously labeled "*belief, conjecture, guess, doubt, wavering, distrust, disbelief,* etc." (4.16.661–63).

Although Locke was aware of the mathematical theory of probability formulated by Pascal, he nowhere alludes to it in his writings. Both Locke's exposure to probability theory and his failure to refer to it have been frequently noticed. Two instances here may suffice. Ian Hacking alludes to the matter in discussing Pascal's wager: "Locke picked up Pascal's argument, like much else, from the Port Royal argument. (Indeed it has regularly been conjectured that Locke was one of the 'several hands' who translated one of the early English editions.)" After briefly touching on Locke's version of the argument, he concludes, "Locke, it is evident, had no conception of probability logic" (*Emergence* 70). Douglas Patey follows much the same line: "It has often been remarked that nowhere in his discussion of probability does Locke make reference to the new mathematical theory of chances, nor does he even quantify probability, as does the Port-Royal *Logic.* . . . It is impossible that Locke was unaware of these developments, and unlikely that the student of Wallis was so hampered by his much remarked on improficiency in mathematics as not to understand them" (33). My suggestion for this reticence has to do with Locke's ideas concerning the value of mathematical demonstration. For Locke, the power of mathematics consists of deductive demonstrations that result in certain knowledge. He does not recognize the validity of an inductive mathematics whose results cannot guarantee exactness. Thus, as Patey writes, "Locke deplores any attempt to quantify probability as he conceives it" (33):

> The difficulty is, when Testimonies contradict common Experience, and the reports of History and Witnesses clash with the ordinary course of Nature, or with one another; there it is, where Diligence, Attention, and Exactness is required, to form a right Judgment, and to proportion the *Assent* to the different Evidence and Probability of the thing. . . . These are liable to so great variety of contrary Observations, Circumstances, Reports, different Qualifications, Tempers, Designs, Over-sights, *etc.* of the Reporters, that 'tis impossible to reduce to precise Rules, the various degrees wherein Men give their Assent. (*Essay* 4.16.663)

Patey's reading of this passage leads him to the conclusion that Craige's attempt to quantify probability as defined by Locke violates Locke's own conception of probable knowledge. Such, however, is not the case. Immediately following Locke's conclusion that "'tis impossible to reduce [probability] to precise Rules," he notes an exception. There is, says Locke, one universally approved rule of evidence of English law, that though the attested copy of a record is admissible, a copy of a copy can never be admitted into evidence (cf. Phipson 754). The argument Locke generates from this in the *Essay* is the source for Craige's argument concerning the diminishing credibility of the Gospel:

> This practice, if it be allowable in the Decisions of Right and Wrong, carries this Observation along with it, *viz.* That any Testimony, the farther off it is from the

original Truth, the less force and proof it has. The Being and Existence of the thing it self, is what I call the original Truth. A credible Man vouching his Knowledge of it, is a good proof: But if another equally credible, do witness it from his Report, the Testimony is weaker; and a third that attests the Hear-say of an Hear-say, is yet less considerable. So that *in traditional Truths, each remove weakens the force of the proof:* And the more hands the Tradition has successively passed through, the less strength and evidence does it receive from them. This I thought necessary to be taken notice of: Because I find amongst some Men, the quite contrary commonly practised, who look on Opinions to gain force by growing older; and what a thousand years since would not, to a rational Man, contemporary with the first Voucher, have appeared at all probable, is now urged as certain beyond all question, only because several have since, from him, said it one after another. Upon this ground Propositions, evidently false or doubtful enough in their first beginning, come by an inverted Rule of Probability, to pass for authentick Truths; and those which found or deserved little credit from the Mouths of their first Authors, are thought to grow venerable by Age, and are urged as undeniable.

I would not be thought here to lessen the Credit and use of History. . . . But this, Truth it self forces me to say, That no Probability can arise higher than its first Original. What has no other Evidence than the single Testimony of one only Witness, must stand or fall by his only Testimony, whether good, bad, or indifferent; and though cited afterwards by hundreds of others, one after another, is so far from receiving any strength thereby, that it is only the weaker. . . . This is certain, that what in one Age was affirmed upon slight grounds, can never after come to be more valid in future Ages, by being often repeated. But the farther still it is from the Original, the less valid it is, and has always less force in the mouth, or writing of him that last made use of it, than in his from whom he received it. (4.16.663–65)

Craige's argument does not (as Patey contends it does) attempt to reduce probability as defined by Locke to precise rules, but instead develops a mathematical demonstration of the diminution of such a probability based on a universally approved rule of evidence. Like Locke, Craige never recognized the validity of inductive probability theory. As mentioned above, the chapter on mathematics he contributed to Wotton's comparison of ancient and modern learning omits any mention of the mathematical theory of probability, although his purpose in the chapter was to champion the superior innovations introduced by the moderns. Wotton's own comments underline the perceived distinction between the certain demonstrations of mathematics and the opinions of probability: "But for the Precedency in those Parts of Learning which still remain to be enquired into, *the Moderns* have put in their Claim, with great Briskness. Among this Sort, I reckon Mathematical and Physical Sciences, considered in their largest Extent. These are things which have no Dependence upon the Opinions of Men for their Truth; they will admit of fixed and undisputed Mediums of Comparison and Judgment" (78). Craige's demonstration of the wager argument in the *Theology* is entirely geometric in nature. Ian Hacking smiles in passing at Craige's "travesty" of Pascal's wager argument (*Emergence* 72); Patey, who at least recognizes that

Craige's source is not Pascal, but Locke, endorses Hacking's view that Locke's version of the wager demonstrates that he "had no conception of probability logic" (Hacking, *Emergence* 70; cf. Patey 33). The absence of the probability calculus in the works of Locke and Craige is not evidence of their ignorance, but rather testimony to their rejection of its inductive method as insufficient. They would consider the versions of the wager argument that they offer more valid than that presented by Pascal, precisely because they avoid his "doctrine of chances" in favor of a Newtonian method of deductive demonstration proceeding from "universally acknowledged" hypotheses.

For both Locke and Craige, what links the wager argument with the argument for historical skepticism is the common theme of prudent judgment. Their versions of the wager argument, like Pascal's, emphasize the faculty of prudent judgment in choosing a course for belief based on rational expectations. The distinction between Pascal's use of induction on the one hand and the more cautious Newtonian method on the other is important for what it says about different views concerning the role of prudence. While the inductive method provides only an approximate, probable guide, the Newtonian method, granted certain "universally acknowledged" hypotheses never contradicted by experiment, claims the force of certain demonstration. It is because of this that Locke could envision a "Morality as capable of Demonstration as Mathematicks." His argument convicts those who disbelieve of "a most manifest wrong Judgment"; Craige, who wrote in order that men may "pursue their pleasures prudently," concludes that "atheists and deists are the most foolish of all foolish men" (Appendix 71, 83). The theme of prudence is also current in Locke's argument for historical skepticism. The faculty of prudence requires a "right Judgment" of the past, and it is to assist in forming this judgment that Locke offers his argument. Certainly, Craige exploits this theme of prudence in his theological application. His evaluation of the past, far from leading him to the conclusion that faith was almost gone (as his opponents repeatedly implied), led him to condemn the folly and false judgment of his millenarian contemporaries. His rational calculations indicate that belief will not disappear before 3150, "whence it is clear how seriously mistaken are all those who establish the advent of Christ so near to our own times" (Appendix 70).

If both Locke and Craige emphasize the need for prudence and "right Judgment" in "this fleeting state of Action and Blindness we are in" (Locke, *Essay* 000), then so too did both men look to mathematics as a sober and steady guide. Craige writes, "it seems absurd not to be able to extend the usefulness of mathematics, 'the divine science,' beyond the narrow boundaries of this life. As the whole world of nature is made stable by geometric laws, how can anyone doubt that these lead us on to the knowledge of nature's omniscient Creator?" (Appendix 53).[9]

It is in some respects surprising then that the most extended criticism of Craige's treatise came from another Newtonian, Humphrey Ditton. This popularizer of Newton's *Principia* attacked Craige at some length in his *Discourse Concerning the Resurrection of Jesus Christ,* and his criticisms formed the basis for all subsequent responses. Consisting of two propositions spanning nine pages, Ditton's argument may be summarized as follows. He first proposes that when we speak of a decrease in credibility, we should distinguish the cause of such a decrease as being due either to "the loss or want of some of those Conditions which first made it (rationally) credible" (162), or to the unwillingness of the auditor to believe:

> This may arise from several Causes; which lying all within ourselves, we ourselves are responsible for all the consequences of it, as far forth as we have contributed to it by any sort of irrational Management. If we make a Testimony less credible to ourselves by any wrong Notions or Hypothesis, by slight and superficial Consideration, or Neglect and Disregard of any of the material Circumstances of it, the Blame of this redounds to ourselves; and it would be absurd for us to cry out in such a Case, That the Credibility of this Testimony is almost dwindled away. (163)

Ditton next proposes that there can never be a "Decrease of the Probability or Credibility of Testimony" so long as witnesses are assumed to be "faithful, careful, and knowing" (164). From this proposition, he draws two corollaries. The first of these is to the effect that all calculations (like Craige's) that are not based on the reliability of witnesses are to be rejected: "No Calculation of the Decrease of the Credibility of Testimony wherein at least a Man pretends to talk of the World of Realities, and not of the meer Fictions of his own Brain, can ever proceed upon any other Principle, than that of the Characters and Qualifications of the Witnesses" (165).

The second corollary consists of three scholia, of which the first is to the effect that time alone cannot diminish the evidence that supported the original testimony. He then considers, in the second scholium, "the Difference between real Evidence, or the just and true Grounds for the Belief of an History, at any time, and the sensible Impression or Influence which that History may have to make upon Men's Minds" (168). While time cannot diminish evidence, it does diminish this "sensible impression." Ditton then argues "That some Matters of Fact may be . . . all things considered, more credible to those who live in remoter Ages" (171). His reasoning here (against Locke's general argument as well as Craige's specific version) is that not only does the evidence itself remain as strong as made the original testimony credible, but in the intervening years, many thousands have "voted it a rationally credible Testimony," thereby adding "a considerable Value and force to the Proof itself" (170).

Probability, as defined by Locke and Craige, is determined by the individual—it corresponds to the degree to which an auditor believes a historical account.

This usage emphasizes the sense of credibility. For Ditton, on the other hand, probability is determined by the text itself—it corresponds to the degree of plausibility that the historical account possesses. This usage emphasizes the sense of the authority rather than the credibility of a text. Thus, Ditton is able to argue that probability diminishes only as the authority of a witness or his account is impugned. Moreover, he can claim that the common acceptance of a history lends further credence to the original, because the growing audience indicates the work's increasing authority and consequently its increasing probability. Such an argument assumes, a priori, that belief is an effect of reason: "No Testimony is really, and in the Nature of things, rendered less credible by any other Cause, than the loss or want of some of those Conditions which first made it (rationally) credible in such or such a Degree" (136). Locke's definition of probability, on the other hand, arose out of an attempt to account for how man believes, that is, how he exercises his faculty of judgment: "*Probability* . . . is enough to induce the Mind to *judge* the Proposition to be true" (*Essay* 4.15.654).

The idea that probability was determined by the text's authority was not merely the property of those, like Ditton, who assumed belief was based on reason. John Edwards responded to what he took to be Craige's argument that "there is only a probability of the truth of the Christian Religion" (85). Like Ditton, Edwards considers the probability of a text an attribute of the text itself, not of the reader of the text; for Edwards, the authority of the Gospel compels the belief of the reader. What typifies Augustan considerations of probability is neither one view nor another, but a confusion that allows Locke and Craige to use "probability" in one sense while their answerers use it in another.

In attempting to locate Locke's contribution to the Augustan concept of probability, Patey focuses on Locke's labeling all evidence as testimony (evidence of fact is testimony of the senses). He interprets this labeling as following the Renaissance concept of probability, comparing Locke's ideas to those in Coke's *Art of Logick* of 1654 (cf. Patey 21–24). Locke's crucial departure from previous thought, however, is that he equates probability not with *force of* testimony, but with *belief in* testimony. In doing so, he shifts the issue from a concern with the authority of a text to a concern with the reader's judgment of that text. Where Coke's canons give fixed rules for determining degrees of assent (i.e., "Publicke testimonies of publick seals are firm" [163]), Locke only enumerates those factors that are "to be considered" in forming a judgment. Directly contradicting the use of canons such as those provided by Coke, Locke writes, "'tis impossible to reduce to precise Rules, the various degrees wherein Men give their Assent" (*Essay* 4.16.663). Patey appears to err when he asserts that the factors Locke lists "are fully traditional canons" (24).[10] In fact, they are not canons at all, for they make no evaluative claim; on the contrary, Locke explicitly rejects the notions of canons.

Ian Hacking is much nearer the mark in distinguishing modern probability by what he terms its duality: "It has to do both with stable frequencies and with degrees of belief" (*Emergence* 10). A corollary to this observed duality is the need for induction. A mathematical calculus of probability (like all inductive demonstrations) may be described as a belief based on, and correlated to, an observed stable frequency. In this respect it serves as a model for the faculty of prudence. Yet it would be wrong to assume that such a notion of probability simply replaced previous notions; instead, the earlier notion survived side by side with the newer notion.[11]

A special value in studying this changing notion of probability—and particularly the minor controversy involving Locke, Craige, Ditton, and others—is what it illustrates in the way of a crisis about the nature of belief at the end of the seventeenth century. The confusion of terms and usages reveals nothing so clearly as a crisis over where belief resides. Is it an attribute of the text itself, to be apprehended in the same degree by every reasonable reader, or is it at the discretion of the reader, to be portioned out according to the dictates of his or her individual judgment?

Barbara Shapiro, in tracing the seventeenth-century development of a theory of evidence in law, observes how the "older notions continued to jostle the new" (186). When it became clear after the 1679 conviction of the Earl of Stafford that most of the peers who convicted him did not believe the witnesses "who swore treason against him," Judge North "expostulated with some of them" as to how they could have found him guilty. They replied that they were "not free" and had been "bound to judge according to the proof of the facts." Since the witnesses had "sworn the facts," they felt they had no choice but to accept them. Judge North informed them that "it is the proper business of peers and juries to try not the grammatical construction of words . . . but the credibility of persons and things . . . if you believe the witnesses find, else not" (qtd. in Shapiro 186).

Here is a clear instance of the confusion over probability and belief. According to Judge North, "the proper business of peers" is to judge according to whether or not they believe. According to the peers, however, a sworn testimony is by its nature a highly probable text and they must submit their belief to its authority. Judge North sentenced the Earl to be executed, thinking his peers believed him guilty, when in fact they did not believe the testimony against him, but felt obligated to acquiesce to the authority of the oath.

Such a confusion may in part explain the phenomenal success of the perjuror Titus Oates. Prior to 1691, only prosecution witnesses could be sworn, so that if a jury was of the same predisposition as the peers who convicted the Earl of Stafford, the defendant was battling against an overwhelming presumption: "Only after 1691 could defense witnesses in treason trials be sworn. This privilege was extended to all felonies in 1707" (Shapiro 186). It has often been remarked that when Oates was first called to tell his story before the King and justices, it was only at his own insistence that his testimony was sworn. Commonly, historians remark on this as indicative of Oates's singular audacity in needlessly exposing himself to the charge of perjury. Yet, under the conditions, his action actually made his own testimony more credible and at the same time less vulnerable to a direct refutation. When, at his trial, the lawyer Richard Langhorn "indicated that his 'whole Defense must run to disable the witnesses,' and that he could 'have no defense unless it be by lessening their Credit,' Lord Chief Justice North advised him: 'Do lessen it if you can'" (Shapiro 185). Under such circumstances, it is hardly surprising that the innocent Langhorn wound up disembowelled.

Not to be overlooked in this confusion over belief is the lament by the peers that they were "not free." Tied up with the question of whether belief resides in the text or the reader is the question of individual liberty. For Locke and Craige, who assert the natural right of individual liberty, belief resides in the reader. For the peers and Humphrey Ditton, however, who were constrained by a higher authority, belief is compelled by the text itself.

This review of the specific philosophical context of Craige's *Theology* has led us to a series of related observations. Craige's argument was not merely, as Hacking says, a travesty of Pascal's wager, but in fact made substantial claims for being taken seriously. The competition that developed in the latter half of the seventeenth century between probability logic and the Newtonian method reveals a fundamental disagreement concerning methods of demonstration. Whether proceeding by strictly inductive or by Newtonian methods, however, probability demonstrations served as a guide for prudent decision-making in moral arguments. The disagreement over method, however, reveals a crisis in the nature of belief: is it an attribute of the text or of the reader? Finally, such a crisis has implications for notions of identity and liberty.

It has been easy to mock the *Theology,* and I would be the last to claim that the work is not bizarre. Yet modern accounts—such as those of Hacking and Patey—dismissing the work as a travesty of Pascal's wager fall into the same error as Lubbock and Drinkwater in the nineteenth century who dismissed the work as "an insane parody of Newton's *Principia.*" The ad hominem assumption behind these appraisals—that Craige was at best an eccentric, and at worst a fool—does not hold up under examination. Just as his other works attest to a significant intellectual competence, a careful study of his argument reveals the pervasive influence of John Locke. If one wishes to attribute Craige's argument to a species of individual folly, then a significant portion of that folly must be traced to Locke. A more plausible explanation of the work accounts for it as a kind of social folly, addressing issues and possibilities that, whatever their appearance today, were important in their own time. Such an explanation is corroborated by the serious reception the work received.

In attempting to treat these issues seriously and sort out the confusion that surrounded ideas of probability, we have been forced to confront (and to a degree, modify) modern theories of the history of probability logic. Where Hacking and Patey argue that Locke "had no conception of probability logic," I have tried to show that (like Craige) he consciously avoids endorsing the inductive method. Instead, both men proceed according to a Newtonian method that begins with an analysis of particular events, generalizes by careful induction to a hypothesis, and from such principles derives a demonstration through deductive reasoning. The purpose of such a method was to keep the use of induction to a minimum and use hypotheses only so long as they could be confirmed experientially.

Newton maintained that if one could contradict his hypotheses by experiment he would revise them and the demonstrations derived from them, but as long as experience confirmed these principles, the arguments derived from them had all the force of geometric demonstration. This is the method followed by Craige in the *Theology* and explains why he titled his work in imitation of Newton's *Principia*. The rule of evidence concerning a copy of a copy was induced from the practice of common law. As it is a rule "universally approved," it is the equivalent of a Newtonian principle—a general rule induced from past experience, nowhere contradicted. From this principle Craige deduces his argument. Such a demonstration is consistent with Locke's assertion that "Morality is as Capable of Demonstration as Mathematicks"; at the same time, it differs significantly from the "Doctrine of Chances" practiced by the followers of inductive probability logic.

Whichever method of demonstration one brought to questions of probability, there was a common aim: to discover a guide to prudent action, based on an evaluation of known occurrences. The difference between the two methods was essentially a difference between product and process; induction focuses on the choice one should make, while the Newtonian method emphasizes the act of choosing. The emphasis in Pascal's version of the wager is on whether one should submit to a belief in God; in the versions articulated by Locke and Craige, the emphasis is on right judgment—the process of choosing wisely and reasonably. For Pascal, the goal is a truth that can only be educed; for Locke and Craige, the goal is a reliable guide that, from cautiously induced principles, can provide certain demonstration.

These differences lead to considerable confusion over the synonomous terms *credibility, probability,* and *belief* that reveals a crisis in the nature of belief. Is belief an attribute of the text or of the reader? Ditton writes, "Persons would do well, when they talk of the vanishing Credibility of Testimony, to tell whether they mean it is become less credible in itself, (that is really less deserving of Credit and Belief) or only less credible in the Notions of the Person, to whom the Testimony is proposed, or by whom it is considered" (165). Ditton dismisses all arguments for the latter alternative, "the very Foundation of them being totally wrong" (165). While Ditton conceives of belief as an attribute of the text, compelling all rational readers to the same degree, Locke and Craige, on the other hand, defining probability as "the agreement or disagreement of . . . ideas" (*Essay* 4.15.654; Appendix 55), locate belief within the mind of the individual. Such a crisis places under stress the notion of personal identity. The more traditional view grants authority to the text and compels the belief of a reader who is "not free," while the Lockean view locates belief in consciousness, which is for Locke the definition of self. Belief is free, determined not by the text, but by the reader's judgment of the text.

APPENDIX

NOTES

WORKS CITED

INDEX

The Mathematical Principles
of
Christian Theology

by
John Craige

Translated from the original Latin by Richard Nash

To the Reverend
Lord Gilbert
[Burnet]
by Divine Providence,
Bishop of Salisbury
and secretary of the
Order of the Garter,
this Treatise
in Theology
is most humbly dedicated by
Jo. Craig.

Preface to the Reader

I AM WELL AWARE THAT I WILL BE UNDERTAKING SOMETHING STRANGE AND difficult when I try to reduce to geometric laws things so far removed from the senses. But I have given serious thought to the outstanding advances in natural sciences that ancient and modern mathematicians have deduced and demonstrated from geometry. These advances have made me hope that the same methods might be of some use in theological matters. It seems absurd not to be able to extend the usefulness of mathematics, "the divine science," beyond the narrow boundaries of this life. As the whole world of nature is made stable by geometric laws, how can anyone doubt that these lead us on to the knowledge of nature's omniscient Creator? The more thoroughly we understand any branch of knowledge, the better we are able to appreciate and measure our Maker's power and wisdom. When asked what God did, that divine philosopher Plato made the excellent answer, "God geometrizes." And for this reason he quite properly excluded from his circle of students in philosophy all those ignorant of geometry. It is an empty philosophy that does not lead us to the knowledge of nature and her author, and any knowledge of either one that we may hope to draw from any source other than geometry is, to say the least, sterile. This most noble science has such broad applicability that it lends itself uncommonly well even to establishing the probability of revealed religion (i.e., faith). I trust that my readers will find this done, to their complete satisfaction, in what I am publishing here. They will find, however, that I treat only the general principles of religion, especially those that I considered as establishing Christianity's teachings and confirming our hope of a life to come. I judge this the more imperative as the assaults of atheists and deists against the truth of our religion grow stronger. I am not making it my concern to inquire what the particular causes of this raging atheism may be; I only propose to supply, if I can, some remedy for the deadly disease.

I am sure that some readers, led by more zeal than common sense, will condemn my efforts out of hand, rashly leaping to the conclusion that I am destroying religion rather than building it up. Those who accept completely all the dogmas of religion will doubtless think that I am undertaking something unsuitable to Christianity in trying to demonstrate its probability. To these I say only that, being preoccupied with their prejudices, they have not yet examined carefully

Translator's note: Translation is from the 1699 edition of *Theologiae Christianae Principia Mathematica* by John Craige and has been checked against the 1755 edition, edited by J. Daniel Titius, and an anonymous partial translation published in 1964 as "Craig's Rules of Historical Evidence," *History and Theory,* Beiheft 4. All endnotes in the text are mine.

enough the foundations of the religion that they profess; and that they do not rightly understand the nature of faith, which is so much praised in Holy Scripture. For faith is nothing other than that persuasion of the mind, derived from an indeterminate probability, by which we believe certain propositions to be true. If the persuasion arises from certainty, then it is not faith that is being produced, but knowledge. Probability generates faith, but destroys knowledge; certainty, on the other hand, generates knowledge and destroys faith. Thus, knowledge removes every occasion for doubt, while faith leaves always a certain hesitation in the mind. That is the reason that faith is distinguished with so many praises and has so many rewards joined to it: that in spite of all the doubts that trouble them, men may walk in the path of virtue and piety, endeavoring with all their might to do what they think will please their omnipotent Creator. They show themselves so ready to obey divine commands of any kind that they are unwilling to reject even those that only probably proceed from God.[1]

I anticipate only two objections of any substance. The first is that I fail to define accurately the time at which the probability of the history of Christ ought to be disappearing, because I take this probability as always decreasing at a certain regular rate, without considering that new degrees of probability will arise from the fulfillment of certain prophecies. But the answer is easy: I have only considered this history of Christ the Savior as it has been transmitted up to this point through so many centuries. If my calculus assumed the fulfillment of those prophecies, I would be unfairly postulating the answer that is being sought. New degrees of probability arising from the fulfillment of prophecies will not matter much, except for the men of the century in which the event answers the prediction. They certainly will not be enough to impair or destroy my calculus.

A more formidable appearance is presented by the second objection, that is, that my calculus seems to weaken the authority of Moses and of other Old Testament authors. I grant this: their authority would indeed have been done with many centuries ago, if Christ's advent had not added a new probability to them. The Son of man came in order to fulfill the law and the prophets, to restore their probability as it was on the point of completely vanishing. Therefore, my calculus builds up Christianity on firm foundations and at the same time destroys the foundations of Judaism.

Definitions

1. Pleasure is that agreeable mental sensation produced in us by objects suitable.
2. The intensity of pleasure is its magnitude, to be determined from the magnitude of that agreeable mental sensation.

3. The duration of pleasure is the length of time that that agreeable mental sensation prevails.
4. Uniform pleasure maintains the same degree of intensity throughout its duration.
5. Pleasure uniformly increasing has its degrees of intensity uniformly increasing throughout the particular moments of its duration.

Note. From their infinite variety of increasing and decreasing degrees of intensity, some species of pleasure are defined as infinite.

6. Probability is the appearance of agreement or disagreement between two ideas through arguments whose logical connection is not certain, or at least is not perceived to be so.
7. Natural probability is that which is deduced from arguments conformable to our own observation or experience.
8. Historical probability is that which is deduced from the testimony of others who testify to their observation or experience.
9. Suspicion of historical probability is a moving of the mind toward contrary versions of history.
10. Velocity of suspicion is the force by which the mind at a certain time is driven as if through a kind of space toward contrary versions of history.

Note. By space, I understand here the amount of assent that the mind yields to contrary arguments of a history. Obviously I conceive the mind as a movable and arguments as moving forces driving it one way or the other.

Axioms

1. Every man strives to produce pleasure in his mind, to increase or continue in his state of pleasure.
2. The efforts of wise men are in direct proportion to the true value of their expectations. The wisest man aims at such a proportion in his efforts; and anyone who aims at this less carefully is judged to be less wise.
3. The efforts of the foolish are in inverse proportion to the true value of their expectations.

This axiom is not to be understood in a mathematically rigorous way. I wish only to give a hint of it here, because those men employ greater efforts toward obtaining an expectation whose true value is a than they do toward obtaining some other hope whose true value is na where n is assumed to be greater than one.

Hypothesis

All men have an equal right to be believed unless the contrary has been somehow established. The justice of this hypothesis is founded on this: that all things of the same nature are endowed with the same natural qualities, whether of mind or body, and it is the common practice of mankind, in any business transacted in this life, to accept any man as a witness unless he has somehow lost this natural right.

1

On Historical Probability Transmitted Orally

HISTORICAL PROBABILITY IS DIMINISHED FROM THREE SOURCES ESPECIALLY: the number of witnesses through whom the testimony is successively transmitted; the distance of the place from which the subject is reported (but this concerns only those histories whose principal subjects are permanent, for if they are transient, probability is not at all diminished by distance of place), and the length of time through which the history is transmitted. The rate by which probability decreases in some particular examples will be demonstrated in the following propositions. Some other causes of diminishing historical probability I do not consider here, as they are of little importance and do not destroy the force of my principal conclusions. They can be reduced to a calculus from the principles here laid down.

Proposition 1   Theorem 1

Any history whatsoever (that is not contradictory) confirmed by the testimony of a single original witness has a degree of probability.

A great probability is made up from many testimonies of prime witnesses, just as a great number is made up from many units. It is possible, indeed, to have a degree of probability so slight that our mind can scarcely perceive it, just as in the motion of bodies there can sometimes be so small a degree of velocity that we cannot discern the motion with our eyes. But that small degree of probability is of a determinable size, just like the comparable degree of velocity, and if repeated many times it produces a perceptible probability.

Proposition 2   Theorem 2

Historical probability increases by the number of prime witnesses who narrate the fact.

A single witness produces a single degree of probability (by proposition 1). Therefore, two witnesses produce two degrees of probability, three witnesses three degrees, and so on. Q.E.D.

Corollary. Let there be any history H, related by a number of prime witnesses $n + m$, to a man A, a certain number of which witnesses, n, narrate the same event to another man B; then the probability that A has will be to the probability B has as $n + m$ is to n.[2] So that if, for example, $n = 4$, $m = 8$, the probability that A has will be triple the probability that B has.

Proposition 3   Theorem 3

Suspicions of a historical probability always transmitted by a single witness (other things being equal) increase in proportion to the number of witnesses through whom the history is transmitted.

Let s be the total suspicion that we have concerning the trustworthiness and other virtues of a perfect witness. Then if one witness yields s, two witnesses will yield $2s$, three witnesses will yield $3s$, and the total number of witnesses n will yield suspicion ns, for s is the same in each man (by the hypothesis).

Corollary. Let M be the number of witnesses through whom a history is successively transmitted, then $(M - 1)s$ will be the total suspicion transmitted to the last witness, for he will have the suspicions due to all witnesses except that arising from his own relation, which he does not transmit to himself.

Proposition 4   Lemma 1

The velocities of suspicion produced over equal spans of time increase in arithmetical progression.

In the first figure, let AF be the time through which a given history is transmitted; let it be supposed to be divided into the very small and equal parts AB, BC, CD, DE, EF. And let the line Bb at right angles to the said AF be the velocity arisen from the small space of time AB. I maintain that at the end of the next space of time BC, the velocity of suspicion will be $Cc = 2Bb$, and that at the end of the third space of time CD, the velocity of suspicion will be $Dd = 3Bb$, and so on.

For a history transmitted through a period of time, BC will have a suspicion Cx ($= Bb$) even if every cause of suspicion ceases to operate; therefore, when the same cause of suspicion is operative through the period of time BC that was

Figure 1

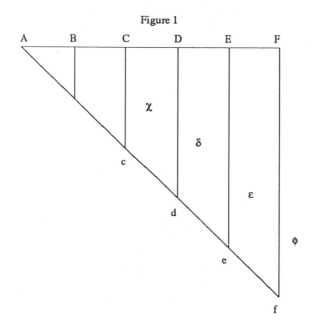

operating through the period of time AB, the velocity Cx will be increased by the quantity $Xc = Bb$, because the periods of time are equal and the cause of suspicion is supposed to be a uniform force. Thus, the velocity of suspicion at the end of the period of time following BC will be $Cc = C + c = 2Bb$. Likewise, if at time C every cause of suspicion should cease, the history would proceed with the suspicion conceived in C, that is, when carried on to D its velocity will be $D\delta$ $= Cc = 2Bb$. Therefore, allowing for the same uniform cause of suspicion through time CD as through the equal period of time AB, the velocity of suspicion D will be increased by the quantity $\delta d = Bb$. Accordingly, at time D the velocity of suspicion will be $Dd = D\delta + \delta d = 3Bb$. Likewise, if at time D all cause of suspicion should cease, the history would proceed with the suspicion conceived in D, that is, when carried on to E its velocity would be $E\varepsilon = Dd = 3Bb$. Therefore, allowing for the same uniform cause of suspicion through time De as through the equal time AB, the velocity E will be increased by the quantity $\varepsilon e = Bb$. Hence the velocity of suspicion at time E will be $Ee = E\varepsilon + \varepsilon e = 4Bb$. Finally, with every cause of suspicion ceasing in E, the history will proceed with the velocity of suspicion conceived in E.[3] That is, carried on to F, its velocity will be $F\phi = Ee = 4Bb$. Therefore, allowing for the same uniform cause of suspicion through final time EF as through the first and equal time AB, the velocity of suspicion $F\phi$[4] will be increased by the quantity $\phi f = Bb$, and thence the entire velocity at time F will be $Ff = F + \phi f = 5Bb$. It follows that in the equal times AB, BC, CD, and so on, the velocities of suspicion Bb, $2Bb$, $3Bb$ are in simple arithmetical progression. Q.E.D.

Proposition 5   Theorem 4

Suspicions of the probability of a history transmitted through any length of time (other things being equal) increase in square ratio[5] to the time passed since the beginning of the history.

Let a line $Abcdef$ be drawn through the extremities b, c, d, e, f of the lines Bb, Cc, Dd, Ee, Ff, denoting the degrees of the velocities (all these lines being drawn at right angles to the line designating time AF). The area of the figure AFf will represent the suspicion produced within the time AF, as also the area of ADd will represent the suspicion produced within the time AD, and so for the rest. Now because Bb, Cc, Dd, and so on are in arithmetical progression 1, 2, 3, 4, and so on (by proposition 4), the line $Abcdef$ is therefore straight, as is known from the Elements [of Euclid]. The suspicion produced within the time AF is to the suspicion produced within the time AD as the area of the triangle AFf is to the area of the triangle ADd. But the triangle AFf is to the triangle ADd as the square of the line AF is to the square of the line AD (as is known from the Elements). Therefore, the suspicion arisen within the time AF is to the suspicion arisen within the time AD as the square of the line AF is to the square of the line AD; that is, suspicions are in square ratio to the time passed since the beginning of the history. Q.E.D.

Corollary. Let the time through which the history is transmitted be $AF = T$, and let the suspicion arisen from this be K. Let any other given time be $AD = t$ and the known suspicion arisen from this be k, then the equation will be

$$K = T^2 k / t^2$$

Proposition 6   Theorem 5

Suspicions of the probability of a history transmitted over any distances (other things being equal) increase in square ratio to the distances from the point of origin.

This is demonstrated as with the preceding. Thus, let A be the place at which the subject of the history is reported, and let that history be carried out to any degree of distance $AF = D$, from which arises suspicion Q. When, from any other known distance $AD = d$, some degree of known suspicion be arisen, q, the equation will be

$$Q = D^2 q/d^2.$$

Proposition 7   Problem 1

Determine the quantity of probability of a given history H transmitted on each occasion through a single witness.

Let x denote the entire probability that the first witness can transmit to a second after intervals of time and place as minimal as possible, and let M (or m) denote the number of witnesses through whom in the given time T and to the given distance D that history H is transmitted, and let s be the known suspicion that we posited as arising from any single witness, k the known suspicion posited as arisen from any given time t, and q the known suspicion posited as arisen from any given distance d. Let P be the probability being sought. The equation will be

$$P = x + (m - 1)s + T^2 k/t^2 + D^2 q/d^2.$$

For $(m - 1)s$ is the total suspicion that arises from the number of witnesses (by proposition 3) and $T^2 k/t^2$ is the total suspicion arisen from the given time T (by proposition 5) and $D^2 q/d^2$ is the total suspicion arisen from the distance D (by proposition 6). Therefore, $(m - 1)s + T^2 k/t^2 + D^2 q/d^2$ is the entire suspicion that attaches to the history H transmitted through the number of witnesses M after the elapsed time T and at the distance D. And since x is (from the hypothesis) its total probability at the beginning, it is clear that $P = x + (m - 1)s + T^2 k/t^2 + D^2 q/d^2$. Q. E. D.

Note. Since x designates the entire probability that the first witness transmits to the second, in the number denoted by M that first witness himself is not included; consequently, in what follows we distinguish him from the others by the name of "the historian." By witnesses we understand all those who derive their own knowledge of the history from the observation or experience of the historian.

Example. How much probability has the tenth witness of history H after a lapse of time $10t$ and at a distance $8d$? In this case, $M = 10, T = 10t, D = 8d$; therefore, by the preceding rule, $P = x + 9s + 100k + 64q$ is the probability which the tenth witness has.

It is very important to note that x, s, t, k, d, q must be known quantities, for they are all units necessary to the measuring of probability, which (as in every other kind of measuring) can then be obtained at the will of the measurer.

Proposition 8   Problem 2

Given the number of series of witnesses, the number of historians transmitting the history from the first witness and through whatever series, and likewise for the times and distances through which any history H is transmitted to any man A, find the quantity of probability that A has concerning the truth of history H.

Let the probability be found for any series transmitted separately (by proposition 7), and the sum of all those will be the probability being sought, which is transmitted to A by them all.

Example. Let A receive history H from two series of witnesses. And let b be the number of historians, m the number of witnesses, T the time, and D the distance through which the history is transmitted in its first series. Likewise let c be the number of historians, n the number of witnesses, G the time, and L the distance through which history H is transmitted to A in a second series of witnesses. Now bx is the probability that the first witness has in the first series, and cx is the probability that the first witness has in the second series (by proposition 2). Therefore (by proposition 7), it will be found

Probability transmitted to A through the first series. $\qquad bx + (m-1)s + T^2 k/t^2 + D^2 q/d^2$

Probability transmitted to A through the second series. $\qquad cx + (n-1)s\ G^2 k/t^2 + L^2 q/d^2$

Let these two probabilities be added together, and the sum of the two of them, namely, $bx + cx + [(m-1) + (n-1)]s + (T^2 + G^2)k/t^2 + (D^2 + L^2)q/d^2$, will be the entire probability transmitted to A from the one and the other series.

Corollary. If the number of historians b, the number of witnesses m, the time T, and the distance D are the same in all series of witnesses, the number of which is a, then the probability being sought will be

$$P = a[bx + (m-1)s + T^2 k/t^2 + D^2 q/d^2].$$

And this case I allude to principally in what follows, unless otherwise expressly noted.

Proposition 9   Problem 3

Given a certain history H, find another history h, which, if transmitted by a given number of series of witnesses a, will have a probability in a given proportion to the probability of the given history H.

Let e be the number of series of witnesses, c the number of historians, n the number of witnesses, G the time, and L the distance through which the given history H is transmitted. Let a, b, m, T, D respectively denote the same quantities in the required history h, and let the given proportion be r to 1. Now from the given terms e, c, n, G, L, a, can be discovered b, m, T, D, thus $ecx + (en - e)s + eG^2k/t^2 + eL^2q/d^2$ is the probability of the given history H (by proposition 8, corollary). And $abx + (am - a)s + aT^2k/t^2 + aD^2q/d^2$ is the probability of the history to be found (by proposition 8, corollary). Therefore, it will be

$$abx + (am - a)s + aT^2k/t^2 + aD^2q/d^2 : ecx + (en - e)s + eG^2k/t^2 + eL^2q/d^2 = r{:}1.$$

from the condition of the problem. Therefore, multiplying the middle and extreme terms, it will be

$$abx + (am - a)s + aT^2k/t^2 + aD^2q/d^2$$
$$= recx + (ren - re)s + reG^2k/t^2 + reL^2q/d^2.$$

Comparing parallel terms, it will be $ab = rec$; $am - a = ren - re$; $aT^2 = reG^2$; and $aD^2 = reL^2$. Reducing these will give the equations: $b = rec/a$; $m = (ren - re + a)/a$; $T = \sqrt{reG^2/a}$; $D = \sqrt{reL^2/a}$. Q. E. I.

Note. A history is called given or found when the number of series of witnesses, the number of historians, the number of witnesses, and the distance and time through which the history is transmitted or to be transmitted are given or found.[6]

Proposition 10   Problem 4

Given a certain history H, find another history h that, if transmitted by a given number of historians b, can have a probability in a given proportion to the probability of given history H.

With quantities designated as in the preceding proposition we will have

$$a[bx + (m - 1)s + T^2k/t^2 + D^2q/d^2] = re[cx + (n - 1)s + G^2k/t^2 + L^2q/d^2].$$

Reducing the resulting equations through the comparison of terms, $a = rec/b$ will be the number of series of witnesses, and $m = (nb - b + c)/c$ the number of witnesses, $T = \sqrt{bG^2/c}$ the time, and $D = \sqrt{bL^2/c}$ the distance through which the required history h that is to be found ought to be transmitted, so that its probability may be to the probability of the given history H as r to 1.

Proposition 11   Problem 5

Given a certain history H, find another history h that, if transmitted to a witness appearing in a given sequence m, will have a probability in a given proportion to the probability of the given history H.

Let the quantities be designated as before, then from the given e, c, n, G, L, r, m are to be found a, b, T, D. When equations are reduced through the comparison of terms (as in proposition 9), the number of series of witnesses will be $a = (ren - re)/m - 1$, the number of historians will be $b = (cm - c)/(n-1)$, the time will be $T = G\sqrt{m - 1}/(n - 1)$, and the distance $D = L\sqrt{m - 1}/(n - 1)$ through which the required history h should be transmitted.

Example. Let a given history H be transmitted to the fourth witness by two series of witnesses and by three historians after a hundred years and at a distance of a thousand miles. A history is sought that, when carried on to the fifth witness, will have a probability twice the probability of the given history. In this example, $e = 2, c = 3, n = 4, G = 100, L = 1000, m = 5, r = 2$. With these values substituted for the quantities just now found, $a = 3, b = 4, T = 200\sqrt{1/3}, D = 2000\sqrt{1/3}$.

It follows that history h, carried out to the fifth witness by four historians through three series of witnesses after $200\sqrt{1/3}$ years elapsed and at a distance of $2000\sqrt{1/3}$ miles, will be twice as probable as the given history H.

Proposition 12   Problem 6

Given a certain history H, find another history h that, after the given time T, will have a probability in a given proportion to the probability of history H.

Reducing the preceding equations by comparison of terms you will find the number of series of witnesses $a = reG^2/T^2$, the number of historians $b = cT^2/G^2$, the number of witnesses $m = [(nT^2 - T^2)/G^2] + 1$, and the distance $D = TL/G$ through which the required history h must be transmitted. Since T is given, and a, b, m, D are found, the history h is found (by the note to proposition 9).

Proposition 13 Problem 7

Given a certain history H, find another history h (whose subject is reported with reference to a place), which history, transmitted at a given distance D, will have a probability in a given proportion to the probability of the given history H.

When the preceding equations are reduced by comparison of terms, you will find the number of series of witnesses $a = reL^2/D^2$, the number of historians $b = rD^2/L^2$, the number of witnesses $m = [(nD^2 - D^2)/L^2] + 1$, and the time $T = GD/L$. Q. E. I.

Note. If in any particular example of these problems a, b, or m should be fractional numbers, the whole numbers closest to these fractions are to be used.

Proposition 14 Theorem 6

A historical probability, transmitted from a single historian through a single series of any number of witnesses, may continually decrease, but nevertheless does not at any given time wholly disappear.

Now $x + (m - 1)s + T^2k/t^2 + D^2q/d^2$ is the probability transmitted from a single historian through a single series of witnesses (by proposition 7). But if this probability could disappear in a certain given time T, in this case it would be $x + (m - 1)s + T^2k/t^2 + D^2q/d^2 = 0$. But if this can happen in a particular case, then it is also possible that in that case $a[x + (m - 1)s + T^2k/t^2 + D^2q/d^2] = 0$, however great a number of series of witnesses a is supposed. This is false, for it is possible to assume a number a so large that at the beginning of a history its probability will be greater than any given probability produced by a single historian. But a probability greater than any given will not disappear at any given time; therefore, it is impossible (assuming an extremely large number a) that $a[x + (m - 1)s + T^2k/t^2 + D^2q/d^2] = 0$. Therefore, it is impossible that $x + (m - 1)s + T^2k/t^2 + D^2q/d^2 = 0$. For if the product of two multiplied quantities is greater than nothing, then the individual factors must themselves be greater than nothing, from which the proposition holds true.

Note. Although a historical probability may never absolutely disappear, yet in the process of time it becomes so attenuated that the mind is hardly able to perceive its force. This being so, we still need to demonstrate a method for determining the time in which that degree of probability needed to produce a perceptible force on the mind disappears. To do this as simply as possible, I create the following hypotheses, which I judge to be not far from the truth. 1) $s = -x/10$; that is, a probability transmitted entire from the historian to its first witness produces no perceptible force (other things being equal) in the mind of the eleventh witness. 2) In a space of 50 years $= t$ arises the suspicion $k = -x/100$. For if the first witness, having received the history from the historian himself, transmits it at once to another, he destroys the tenth part of the probability transmitted to himself (by hypothesis 1). Now, if he delay his relation for fifty years, he will destroy a hundredth part of the probability transmitted to him (in addition to that tenth part). 3) At a distance of 50 miles $= d$ arises a suspicion $q = -x/10,000$ in histories whose subjects have reference to a permanent place. 4) The life of any single witness will last for 50 years $= t$. And thus, 5) the number of witnesses through whom a history is transmitted for any length of time T will be $m = T/t$. This follows from the fourth hypothesis.

Proposition 15   Problem 8

To determine when the probability of any kind of history (whose subject is transient), transmitted by word of mouth only, will disappear.

It will disappear when $bx + (m - 1)s + T^2k/t^2 = 0$ (by proposition 8), where b is the number of historians, m the number of witnesses, and T the required time of vanishing probability. Now because $m = T/t$, $s = -x/10$, $k = -x/100$ (by hypotheses 5, 1, 2 of the preceding proposition), substitute these values for the quantities m, s, k; thus $bx - xT/10t + x/10 - xT^2/100t^2 = 0$. Let this equation be reduced by the common rules of algebra, and $T = t\sqrt{100b + 35} - 5t$, the time when the probability of any history disappears.

Corollary. The probability of Christ's history disappeared at the end of the eighth century, insofar as it depended on oral tradition alone. For in this case, $b = 4$, so that $\sqrt{100b + 35} = \sqrt{435} =$ about 21. Therefore, by this proposition $T = 21t - 5t = 16t$, but $t = 50$ years (by hypothesis 2), and therefore $T = 16t = 800$ years. Q. E. D.

In the same way you may find the time for the disappearance of the probability of any history whose subject is permanent; however, you must not take k to have the same quantity in histories with permanent subjects as it has in histories with transient subjects, for it is far greater in the latter than in the former. And because (by hypothesis 2) we have supposed that $k = -x/100$ in histories transmitting transient material, it can happen that in histories transmitting permanent subjects $k = -x/50$, or even less, provided that those permanent subjects be in an accessible place, for if they should be in an inaccessible place their probabilities are to be derived just as if their subjects were transient.

2

On Historical Probability Transmitted Through Written Testimony

Proposition 16   Problem 9

To determine the probability of a history committed to writing by one primary historian.

Let z be the entire probability of a history at the publication of the first text, n the number of texts, T the time, and D the distance, through which the written history is transmitted. And let f be the suspicion arisen from the transcribing of another text (f is the same in all cases, because the transcribers are equally trustworthy, by hypothesis) with other things posited as in the preceding chapter. The probability sought will be

$$P = z + (n - 1)f + T^2 k/t^2 + D^2 q/d^2.$$

Corollary. Let c be the number of primary historians and r the number of secondary texts transmitting the history through however many series, it being posited that each series is derived from only one secondary text. The probability of a history so transmitted will be

$$P = r[cz + (n - 1)f + T^2 k/t^2 + D^2 q/d^2].$$

Note. By primary historians, I mean those who derive their knowledge of a history from their own observation or experience. And by a primary text I mean not one particular text, but any number of texts written or printed by that primary historian. Now since a written history has a far greater probability than a history transmitted orally, and since the latter's probability never disappears (by proposition 14), it follows that the probability of the former never completely disappears at any given time. But since it is continually decreasing, it too must be finally rendered very faint. Therefore, to determine the time at which this perceptible probability perishes, let the following hypotheses be made: 1) that $z = 10x$; that is, the historian transmits ten times greater probability when his testimony is transmitted in writing than when it is transmitted orally; 2) that $f = s/10$;[7] that is, the suspicion of a trustworthy transcriber is only a tenth part of the suspicion of a trustworthy witness, so that it follows that $f = -x/100$ (by proposition 14, hypothesis 1 and hypothesis 2 of this proposition); 3) that a text of a history will last for 200 years $= 4t$. It follows, 4) that the number of texts n transmitting a history through any time T is $n = T/4t$.

Proposition 17   Problem 10

To determine the present probability of a history of Christ written by four historians and transmitted through a single series of texts.

The present probability of the history of Christ is $cz + (n - 1)f + T^2k/t^2$ (by proposition 16, corollary), but in this case the number of primary historians is $c = 4$, $T = 1696$ years $= 34t$. Because (by proposition 16, hypothesis) $z = 10x$, $n = 34/4$, $f = -x/100$, $k = -x/100$, substitute these values for the quantities c, n, f, T. Thus, the present probability of the history of Christ will be

$$P = 40x - 30x/400 - 1156x/100,$$

which being reduced gives

$$P = 11346x/400;$$

that is, approximately $P = 28x$. Therefore, the present probability of the history of Christ is what one would have who, in the times of Christ himself, had received the same history orally from twenty-eight disciples of Christ. Q. E. I.

Proposition 18   Problem 11

To define the time in which the probability of a written history of Christ will disappear.

It will disappear when $cz + (n - 1)f + T^2k/t^2 = 0$ (by proposition 16, corollary); this is (with quantitative values substituted for z, n, f, k, and likewise $c = 4$) when

$$40 + 1/100 - T/400t - T^2/100t^2 = 0.$$

Reducing this equation will give the required time of disappearing probability, namely $T = t\sqrt{4001 + 1/64} - t/8;$[8] or rather (neglecting the fractions, which in such computations may be done without great danger of error) the time sought will be $T = t\sqrt{4001}$, that is, since $\sqrt{4001} = 63$ and $t = 50$ years, $T = 3150$ years. It follows that after 3150 years from the birth of Christ the probability of his written history will disappear. Q. E. I.

Corollary. For Christ to come, 1454 years must first elapse.[9] For it is necessary first that the probability of his history should disappear, but that will come to pass when 1454 years have elapsed since our time ($= 3150 - 1696$); therefore, for him to come, 1454 years must first elapse from our present time. Q. E. D. His coming must occur within no time less than 1454 years, since his advent depends on the disappearance of his history's probability. Many things cause me to suppose that he will not come before his history's probability will have almost disappeared, for Luke 18:8 tells us that Christ said: "Nevertheless, when the Son of man cometh, shall he find faith on the Earth?" Clearly, at the advent of Christ, his history's probability will be so little that he may doubt whether he shall find any man who will repose faith in this, his history. Whence it is clear how seriously mistaken are all those who establish the advent of Christ so near to our own times.

Proposition 19   Problem 12

To determine the probability of any written history according to the hypotheses adopted.

The probability of any written history (whose subject matter is transient) is $P = r[cz + (n - 1)f + T^2k/t^2]$ (by proposition 16, corollary). Therefore, with quantitative values substituted for z, n, f, k it will be

$$P = r(4000ct^2 - Tt + 4t^2 - 4T^2)/400t^2.$$

Proposition 20   Problem 13

To define the period of time in which the probability of a written history of any sort disappears.

It will disappear when $cz + (n - 1)f + T^2k/t^2 = 0$ (by proposition 16, corollary); this is (with quantitative values substituted for z, n, f, k) when $10c + 1/100 - T/400t - T^2/100t^2 = 0$; reducing this equation will give the required time of disappearing probability

$$T = t\sqrt{1000c + 65/64} - t/8;^{10}$$

or with fractions neglected,

$$T = t\sqrt{1000c + 1}.$$

As t is given to be a period of 50 years and c is the number of primary historians, T may therefore be considered the time in which the history's probability disappears.

Note. This same method solves two final problems, when the histories concern subjects situated in an accessible place.

Proposition 21   Problem 14

To determine the probability of a history whose transmission is partly written and partly oral.

Find the probability for the period of time in which it is transmitted orally (by proposition 8) and for the time in which it is transmitted in writing (by proposition 16); the sum of both will give the required probability. Q. E. I.

Proposition 22   Problem 15

Given two opposing histories of the same thing, determine which of these is the more probable and how much its probability is.

Find the probability of each (by propositions 8 and 16) and substitute quantities for m, s, k, q, z, n, f, and at once this will establish which is the more probable; subtract the lesser probability from the greater, and the remainder will be the total probability of the more probable history. Q. E. I.

Conclusion. I believe I have now explained clearly enough all that is necessary for determining historical probability. I proceed now to another portion of my material, namely, defining the quantities of pleasure. For pleasure is the sole principle of all our actions and efforts. Whatever we do or have done to us, whatever we desire or shun, all is for the sake of pleasure. For men to pursue their pleasures prudently, then, they must be able to determine accurately their quantities and values. This will therefore be taught in what follows.

3

On Uniform Pleasure

FOR EASIER DEMONSTRATION OF THE FOLLOWING PROPOSITIONS, I REPRESENT the duration of pleasure by a straight line, and the degrees of its intensity by straight lines perpendicular to individual points of that line. If a line is drawn through the other extremities of these perpendiculars, a plane figure will be formed, which will represent very serviceably the quantity of that pleasure. Thus from the properties of this figure it will be easy to deduce the properties of pleasure.

Proposition 23   Theorem 7

The quantities of two uniform pleasures (whose intensities are equal) are in direct proportion to their durations.

Figure 2

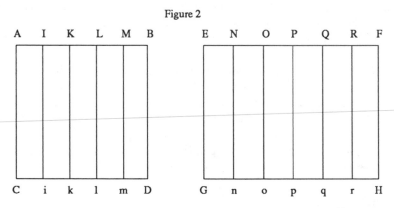

Let AB be the duration of a single pleasure. Let its quantity be v[11] and let AC, Ii, Kk, Ll, and so on be the degrees of intensity at different moments of its duration. And let EF be the duration of another pleasure, its quantity V and the degrees of intensity *EG, Nn, Oo,* and so on at the moments *E, N, O,* and so forth. Since both pleasures are uniform (by hypothesis), a line drawn through *C, i, k, l, m, D* and a line drawn through *G, n, o, p, q, r, H* are straight and parallel to *AB* and *EF* (by definition 4). Therefore, figures *ABCD* and *EFGH* representing the quantity of either pleasure are right angle parallelograms. Now $v = AB \cdot AC$, $V = EF \cdot EG$ (by [Euclid's] Elements), and $AC = EG$ (by the hypothesis of this proposition). Therefore $V = EF \cdot AC$; so that $v{:}V = AB \cdot AC : EF \cdot AC$. So (by the Elements), $AB \cdot AC : EF \cdot AC = AB{:}EF$. Therefore, $v{:}V = AB{:}EF$. Q. E. D.

Proposition 24   Theorem 8

The quantities of two uniform pleasures (whose times of duration are equal) are in direct proportion to their intensities.

Figure 3

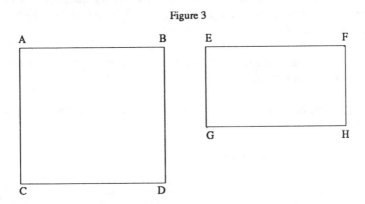

Let the duration of the first pleasure be *AB* and its constant degree of intensity *AC*, the entire quantity equal to *v*. And let the duration of another pleasure be *EF*, its constant intensity *EG*, and its quantity equal to *V*. Then, $v = AB \cdot AC$ and $V = EF \cdot EG$. But by the hypothesis $AB = EF$; therefore $V = AB \cdot EG$, so that $v{:}V = AB \cdot AC : AB \cdot EG$. But $AB \cdot AC : AB \cdot EG = AC{:}EG$. Therefore, $v{:}V = AC{:}EG$. Q. E. D.

Proposition 25   Theorem 9

The quantities of any two uniform pleasures are in direct proportion to their duration and intensity.

Let the duration of a single pleasure be $AB = r$, its intensity $AC = n$, and its

Figure 4

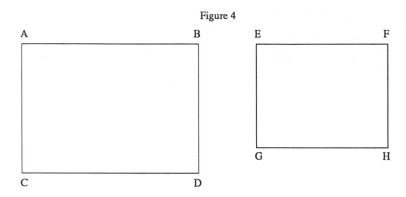

quantity v. And let the quantity of another pleasure be V, its duration $EF = s$, its intensity $EG = m$. Since the figures representing the quantities of uniform pleasures are right angle parallelograms, $v = rn$, $V = sm$. Hence, $V/v = sm/rn = (s/r)(m/n)$. Q. E. D.

Corollary 1. The durations of any two uniform pleasures are as their quantities divided by their intensities.

Corollary 2. The intensities of any two uniform pleasures are as their quantities divided by their durations.

Corollary 3. Any uniform pleasure increases in proportion to the duration since its beginning.

4

On Pleasures Uniformly Increasing

Proposition 26   Theorem 10

The quantities of two pleasures uniformly increasing, with equal intensities at their end are in proportion to their duration.

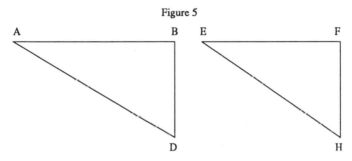

Figure 5

Since the figures representing these pleasures are triangles (by definition 5), let the quantity of one of these be v, the duration $AB = r$, the intensity at the end $BD = n$; let the quantity of another pleasure be V, its duration $EF = s$, and the intensity at the end $FH = m$. Now $V{:}v = EFH{:}ABD$, but $EFH = sm/2$ and $ABD = rn/2$. Therefore, $V{:}v = sm/2{:}rn/2$; whence $V/v = sm/rn$, but $m = n$ (by hypothesis); therefore $V/v = s/r$. Q. E. D.

Proposition 27   Theorem 11

The quantities of two pleasures uniformly increasing, whose durations are equal, are in direct proportion to the intensities at their end.

For with quantities designated as above, it was found that $V/v = sm/rn$, but $s = r$ (by hypothesis); therefore, $V/v = m/n$. Q. E. D.

Proposition 28 Theorem 12

The quantities of any two uniformly increasing pleasures are in direct proportion to their duration and intensity at their end.

For in the next to the last proposition it was shown that $V/v = sm/rn$; that is, $V/v = (s/r)(m/n)$. Q. E. D.

Corollary 1. The durations of two uniformly increasing pleasures are as their quantities divided by their intensities at their end.

Corollary 2. The quantities of a single pleasure, uniformly increasing from its beginning, increase as the square of their durations. Let $AB = T$ be one duration and its quantity at this time Q; let another duration be $AM = t$, and its quantity of pleasure q. Now $Q:q = ABD:AMN$. But $ABD:AMN = ABq:AMq$ (from the Elements); therefore, $Q:q = ABq:AMq$. That is, $Q:q = T^2:t^2$. Q. E. D.

Figure 6

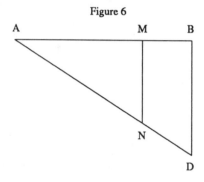

5

On Pleasures Whose Intensities Increase in Some Exponential Ratio

Proposition 29   Problem 16

Given equations expressing the relation between times of duration and degrees of intensity, find the ratio of the quantities of the pleasures.

Figure 7

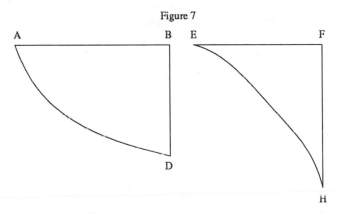

Let the duration of one pleasure be $AB = r$, its intensity at the end $BD = n$, its quantity v, and let the quantity of another be V, its duration $EF = s$, and its intensity at the end $FH = m$. And let $r^c = n$ be the equation expressing the relation between duration and the intensity for the first, increasing in an exponential ratio[12] whose exponent is c. Likewise, let $m = s^e$ be the equation expressing the relation between the duration and the intensity of the second, increasing in an exponential ratio whose exponent is e. Now $V/v = EFH/ABD$ (according to the basis for this method at the beginning of chapter 3). But by the well-known method of quadratures, $EFH = sm/(e + 1)$, $ABD = rn/(c + 1)$. Therefore, $V/v = sm(c + 1)/rn(e + 1) = (s/r)(m/n)(c + 1)/(e + 1)$. That is, the quantities of these pleasures are in direct proportion to their time and intensity (at the end) divided by the exponents increased by one. Q. E. I.

Note. This theorem is of extremely general application for through it one can find out a great many matters concerning pleasures whose intensities increase in exponential ratio. Thus, by positing that $c = 0$, $e = 0$, everything in chapter 3 may be considered demonstrated; if $c = 1$, $e = 1$, everything in chapter 4 may be considered demonstrated. By positing $c = 0$, $e = 1$, one can obtain the ratio of a uniform pleasure to one uniformly increasing, or by positing that $c = 1$, $e = 2$, one can obtain the ratio of a uniformly increasing pleasure to a pleasure whose intensity increases in square ratio to its duration. I shall say nothing of the infinite other cases easily deduced from this proposition.

Proposition 30   Problem 17

With the same givens as in the preceding, find the ratio by which a single pleasure increases with respect to the various times of duration from its beginning.

Figure 8

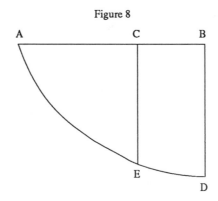

Let Q be the quantity of pleasure produced in the period of time AB, and q the quantity of the same (or similar) pleasure produced in the period of time AC. It may be posited that $AB = T$, $AC = t$. Now $BD = T^c$ and $CE = t^c$ from the hypothesized increase of degrees of intensity; therefore by quadrating you may find that $Q = T^{c+1}/(c + 1) = ABD$, and $q = t^{c+1}/(c + 1) = ACE$. So that $Q/q = T^{c+1}/t^{c+1}$. Q. E. I.

Corollary 1. If the pleasure is uniform, then the quantities of the pleasures will be as the times, for in this case $c = 0$, so that $Q/q = T/t$.

Corollary 2. If the intensities increase uniformly, the pleasures will be as the squares of the times, for in this case $c = 1$, so that $Q/q = T^2/t^2$.

Corollary 3. If the intensities increase as the square of the times, the pleasures will be as the cube of the times, for in this case $c = 2$, so that $Q/q = T^3/t^3$.

Corollary 4. If the intensities increase as the square root of the times, then the quantities of pleasure will be as the square root of the cubes of the times, for in this case $c = \frac{1}{2}$, whence $Q/q = T^{3/2}/t^{3/2} = \sqrt{T^3/t^3}$.

Corollary 5. If the intensities increase as the cube root of the times, then the quantities of pleasure will be as the cube root of the times raised to the fourth power, for in this case $c = \frac{1}{3}$, whence $Q/q = T^{4/3}/t^{4/3} = \sqrt[3]{T^4/t^4}$.

Note. The foregoing establishes how (granting the squaring of curvilinear figures) everything concerning the quantities of pleasures, and the mutual relationships among them, can very easily be found. To clarify this, I supply an example in the following propositions, in which the intensities do not increase in a simple exponential ratio.

Proposition 31   Problem 18

If the intensity increases as the square root of the sum of the square of the duration and the fourth power of the duration are added together, find the ratio by which the pleasure itself increases, with respect to the various times of duration from its beginning.

Figure 9

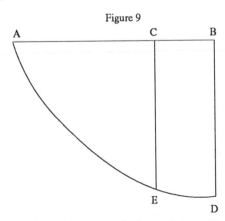

Let $AB = T$ be on duration, $AC = t$ another duration, and let BD be the intensity at the end of the former, and CE the intensity at the end of the latter. Now because $BD = \sqrt{T^4 + T^2}$, $CE = \sqrt{t^4 + t^2}$ (from the hypothesis of the problem, and by the method of quadratics), it is found that $ABD = \frac{1}{3}[(T^2+1)\sqrt{T^2+1}-1] = Q$ and $ACE = \frac{1}{3}[(t^2+1)\sqrt{t^2+1}-1] = q$. Thus,

$$Q/q = [(T^2 + 1)\sqrt{T^2 + 1} - 1]/[(t^2 + 1)\sqrt{t^2 + 1} - 1).$$

For example, let $T = 3\frac{3}{7}$ hours, $t = 2\frac{2}{5}$ hours, $Q/q = 955125/355348.$[13]

Note. Although in the preceding I have supposed the pleasures to be increasing and the intensities at the beginning (except in the case of uniform pleasures) to be indefinitely small, nevertheless the same method can be easily applied to any other pleasures increasing or decreasing by a determined magnitude of intensity, of which an example is given in the following proposition.

Proposition 32   Problem 19

Let AB be the duration of a single pleasure, its intensity at the beginning AC, at the end BD, its quantity v, and let its intensities increase as in the right triangular

Figure 10

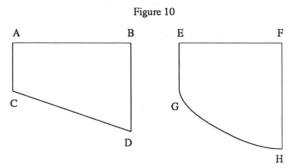

trapezoid $ACBD$. Let the duration of another pleasure be EF,[14] its intensity at the beginning EG, at the end FH, its quantity V, and let its intensities increase as in the right parabolic trapezoid $EFGH$. Find the ratio of the one pleasure to the other.

Let it be posited that $AB = r$, $BD = n$, $AC = t$, $EF = s$, $FH = m$, $EG = g$. From geometry you will find $v = ACBD = (nr + tr)/2$; $V = \frac{2}{3}(mg^2 + ms - g^3)$. Therefore,

$$V/v = (4mg^2 + 4ms - 4g^3)/(3nr + 3tr).\ \text{Q. E. I.}$$

6

On Finite and Infinite Pleasures Compared to One Another

Proposition 33   Theorem 13

A quantity of pleasure having any (nondecreasing) intensity and of infinite duration s is always infinitely greater than some other pleasure having a finite intensity n and of finite duration r.

Suppose that each pleasure is uniform, and V is the quantity of the former, v of the latter. Now $V/v = sm/rn$ (by proposition 25) so that $V = v(sm/rn)$. But s is infinite, and therefore the product sm is infinite; r, n are finite quantities (from the hypothesis). Therefore the product rn is finite, but the infinite quantity sm, divided by the finite quantity rn, gives the infinite quotient sm/rn; therefore $(sm/rn)v$ is an infinite quantity. Therefore V, the quantity of pleasure of infinite duration, is infinitely greater than the quantity of pleasure v, which has a finite intensity and duration. Q. E. D.

Note. Although I have posited uniform pleasures, nevertheless for one who understands the preceding it is clear how to obtain the demonstration of the general argument, when the intensities are assumed to be increasing in any given ratio.

Corollary. The value of the pleasure promised by Christ is infinitely greater than the value of the pleasure of our present life. For the pleasure promised by Christ is of nondecreasing intensity and of infinite duration as is established by his own history, but the pleasure of our present life is of finite intensity and also of finite duration, as is known to all. Therefore, the quantity of the pleasure promised by Christ is infinitely greater than the quantity of the pleasure of our present life (by proposition 33). But the values of pleasures are as their quantities; therefore, the value of the pleasure promised by Christ, etc. Q. E. D.

Proposition 34 Lemma 2

If the probability of obtaining p is in a certain ratio, r to 1, to the probability of obtaining P, and it is supposed that $P>p$ and $r>1$, the true value of one's expectation will be $(P + p)/(r + 1)$; that is, the sum of those things expected divided by the sum of their probabilities, gives the true value of one's expectation.

To understand the demonstration more easily, suppose that a certain person A begins an honest game with another man B. And let x be the wager, or value of A's expectation, and let y be the wager and value of B's expectation (for all players in an honest game have an expectation equal to their wagers), and they play under this condition: that the winner give p to the other, keeping P for himself. Now clearly, if A wins, he will have $x + y - p = P$, but if A loses, then (by the conditions of the game) he will have nothing but p. Now (from the hypothesis of this lemma) A's probability of winning (of obtaining P) is to A's probability of losing (of obtaining p)—that is, to B's probability of winning—in the ratio of 1 to r. Therefore, since the game is supposed honest, the wagers ought to be in the ratio to the probabilities of winning; that is, $x{:}y = 1{:}r$. So, $rx = y$; substituting rx for y in the above equation yields

$$x + rx = P + p.$$

So, $x = (P + p)/(r + 1)$. Q. E. D.

Proposition 35 Theorem 14

The true value of the expectation of obtaining the pleasure P promised by Christ is infinitely greater than the true value of the expectation of obtaining the pleasure p of our present life.

For P is infinitely greater than p (by Proposition 33, corollary), and the probability of obtaining P is indefinite but not inconsiderable (by proposition 17). In addition, the probability of obtaining p is nothing but a finite amount (for life itself is uncertain, and far more so, its pleasure). Therefore, the probability of obtaining p is to the probability of obtaining P is as a finite number to an infinite; therefore, the ratio of these probabilities can be expressed by the ratio of the finite number r to 1. Therefore, the true value of expectation is $(P + p)/(r + 1)$ (by proposition 34). But P is an infinite quantity (by proposition 33, corollary). Therefore, the infinite quantity $P + p$ divided by a finite number, namely $r + 1$, gives an infinite quotient. Therefore, the true value of Christian expectation is in reality infinite; therefore, it is infinitely greater than the true finite value of the expectation of obtaining a pleasure of this present life. Q. E. D.

Corollary 1. Efforts toward obtaining the pleasure of a life to come ought to be infinitely greater than efforts toward obtaining a pleasure of this present life if we wish to govern our efforts wisely (by this and axiom 2).

Corollary 2. Men are foolish who display a greater effort toward obtaining the pleasure of the present life than of the life to come (by this and axiom 3).

Corollary 3. Less wise are those whose efforts toward obtaining the pleasures to come are in finite proportion to their efforts toward finite pleasures (by this and the axioms of chapters 3–6).

Corollary 4. The true Christian is the wisest of all wise men. That atheists and deists are the most foolish of all foolish men follows from corollaries 1 and 2 of this and axioms 2 and 3.

NOTES

1. Responses to Craige's *Theology*

1. Subsequently referred to as the *Theology*. Craige's name is sometimes spelled as "John Craig," but he most often used the final *e*.

2. In his pioneering *History of the Mathematical Theory of Probability from Pascal to Laplace*, Todhunter, acknowledging that he has never read Craige's work, reproduced Lubbock and Drinkwater's remarks. Subsequent accounts, such as that by James McMullen Rigg (J. M. R.) in the *Dictionary of National Biography*, paraphrase their assessment; more recently, J. F. Scott's entry in the *Dictionary of Scientific Biography* avoids the issue by omitting any reference to the *Theology*.

3. In his 1755 edition of the *Theology*, Titius first suggested that the last four chapters were written first without offering any arguments in behalf of this possibility.

4. Todhunter refers to this work as by "Peterson," but it is clear from the context that he has not seen the work himself and is merely quoting from Augustus De Morgan. De Morgan, in turn, is repeating information culled from the pages of *Biographie Universelle*. In doing so, De Morgan errs in transcription, for that work gives the name as "Petersen." A lengthy search under both spellings has failed to turn up evidence that such a work still exists today.

5. "Son opinion est le plus grand example de la vanité des conjectures humaines."

6. "Qua in re maiori adhuc laude dignus esset, si Leibnitii vestigia juvenis legens; eius methodo & signis, recti amore, postea pari, at erga tribules studio, obsecutus Neutono differentialium nomen cum methodo fluxionum senex non commutasset."

7. "Je crois qu'il est impossible d'estimer la probabilité, que donne le temoignage des hommes, soit qu'il soit transmis par la voye orale, ou par l'écriture. C'est pourtant ce qu'a entrepris, & infiniment ou de là un savant Geometre Anglois, dont les manieres honnêtes & obligeantes pour moi m'ont prévenû en faveur de son coeur, autant que ses excellens Ouvrages m'ont donné d'estime pour son esprit. Le livre dont je veux parler a pour titre, *Philosophiae Christianae Principia Mathematica*. Mr. Craige en est l'auteur. Cet Ouvrage est trop curieux pour n'en pas dire ici quelque chose. L'auteur s'y propose principalement de prouver contre les Juifs la verité de l'Histoire de Jesus Christ, & de démontrer aux Libertins que le parti qu'ils prennent de préferer les plaisirs de ce monde si minces & de si courte durée, à l'esperance même incertaine des biens promis à ceux qui suivront la loix de l'Evangile, n'est pas un parti raisonnable ni conforme à leurs vertiables interêts—Mr. Craige à bien vû sans doute que toutes ces consequences n'étoient vrayes qu'en vertû de supposition arbitraires éloignées de la verité peut-être de moitié, du tiers ou du quart, etc. Je dis peut-être, car quel moien de le savoir? il auroit pû en faisant d'autres hypotheses, également vraisemblables, trouver des nombres fort differens. Pour moi je trouve le dessein de Mr. Craige louable & pieux & l'execution aussi heureuse, qu'elle pouvoit l'être; mais je crois cet ouvrage beaucoup plus propre à exercer des Geometres, qu'à convertir des Juifs ou de incredules. Ce que l'on peut conclure de plus certain aprè la lecture de cet ouvrage, c'est que l'Auteur est trés subtile, qu'il est grand Geometre, et qu'il a beaucoup d'esprit."

2. John Craige's Life

1. The biographical information presented in this chapter is based on research (partially funded by a summer faculty fellowship from Indiana University) at the following libraries: University of Michigan; The Burton Historical Collection of the Detroit Public Library; Union Theological Seminary; New York Public Library; British Library; National Library of Scotland; Edinburgh University

Library; Wren Library, Trinity College, Cambridge; the Keynes Collection, King's College, Cambridge; Cambridge University Library; Bodleian Library; Christ Church College Library; Westminster Abbey Library; Salisbury Cathedral Library; Dorset County Record Office; and the Public Record Office.

2. Stone discusses the eroding but still powerful influence of ties of kinship and clientage in Britain in the seventeenth and eighteenth centuries (123–29).

3. The Sacramental Test Act required all holders of civil and military offices to receive the sacrament according to the Anglican rite and to declare their disbelief in transubstantiation.

4. "Habes hic B. L. quae multos ante annos de Calculo fluentium sum meditatus, & cujus prima Elementa, cum Juvenis essem, circa Annum 1685 excogitavi: Quo tempore Cantabrigiae commoratus D. Newtonum rogavi, ut eadem, priusquam praelo committerentur, perlegere dignaretur: Quodq; Ille pro summa sua humanitate fecit: Nec-non ut Objectiones in Schedulis meis contra D. D. T. allatas corroboraret, duarum Figurarum Quadraturas sponte mihi obtulit; erant autem harum Curvarum Aequationes $m^2y^2 = x^4 + a^2x^2$ & $my^2 = x^3 + ax^2$; Meque interim certiorem fecit se posse hujusmodi innumeras exhibere per Seriem Infinitam, quae in datis conditionibus abrumpens Figurae propositae Quadraturam Geometricam determinaret. In Patriam postea redeunti magna mihi intercedebat familiaritas cum Eruditissimo Medico D. Pitcairnio & D. D. Gregorio; quibus significavi qualem pro Quadraturis Seriem haberet D. Newtonus, quam penitus ipsis ignotam uterq; satebatur."

5. For a more detailed account of this incident, see Newton, *Papers* 1:3–6.

6. That Craige viewed this important treatise on method is clear from a comment he makes in passing concerning reducing the root of the integrand to an infinite series: "Juxta Methodum clarissimi viri D. Isaaci Newtoni Geometrae non minus quam Analystae praestantissimi" (*Methodus* 26–27). See Newton, *Papers* 1:3–4.

7. Cohen identifies this copy of the *Principia* (now in the Fisher Library of the University of Sydney, New South Wales, Australia) as Craige's (203–5).

8. "Quam quidem propositionem in construendis navibus non inutilem futuram esse censeo."

9. "Hujus meditationis occasionem ipse praebui, dum Cantabridgiae de Figura navium aptissima invenienda, problema celeberrimo Autori proponerem."

10. The General Scholium that followed Proposition 40 in the manuscript and first edition concludes with a suggestion concerning an inexpensive method for determining the "aptest shape for ships." In subsequent editions, the General Scholium was advanced from section 7 to section 6 of Book 2, and this particular paragraph was deleted.

11. Westfall quotes from a draft of Newton's "observations" on Leibniz's second letter (1716): "Mr. Craige is a witness that in those days I looked upon the method as mine" (719).

12. "Res tanti non est, ut ulteriori disquisitione digna videatur, mihi praesertim qui nec Anglus sum nec Batavus."

13. Jacob explores the relationship of the flourishing of Newtonian science and the ascendancy of Low Church Whig political ideology. Recently, Jacob's thesis has been challenged by Guerrini, who has argued for the existence of a significant circle of Tory Newtonians: "Politically they were Tories. In religion, they were High Church Anglicans who valued the episcopacy and those points of ritual and doctrine that distinguished the English church from nonconformity" (288–89). Guerrini centers this circle around David Gregory and Archibald Pitcairne. In doing so, she illustrates the very real difficulties facing any attempt to define a "Newtonian ideology." In part, as Guerrini suggests (301), these difficulties concern the different connotations surrounding the terms "Whig" and "Tory" in Scotland and England. John Craige and Gilbert Burnet were, in their native land—like their Tory countrymen, Gregory and Pitcairne—Scottish Episcopalians, but in England, where they pursued successful careers, each was a Hanoverian Whig committed to the principles of the Revolution of 1688/89.

14. Foxcroft provides a fairly detailed picture of the church politics during Burnet's tenure as Bishop.

15. Extracts from Craige's letter are published in Newton, *Correspondence* 3:150–51. Brewster published the entire letter in an appendix to volume 1. Westfall succinctly characterizes the task Craige set for Bentley by remarking that his "imposing course of study ought to have frightened anyone away" (504).

16. The wedding itself is recorded as being performed by Mr. John Cleland in the registers of the parish of St. Martin-in-the-Fields. When Craige was installed vicar of Gillingham three years later, "John Cleland of Linwood in the county of Lincolnshire" was one of three men who stood his bond, according to documents in the Public Record Office.

The marriage produced six children, of whom two died in infancy. The eldest was Gilbert, probably named for Bishop Burnet, who was born sometime before Craige became vicar of Gillingham in March of 1696 and who was buried 22 October 1727. Another son, James, was born 24 November 1697 and died in infancy and was buried 4 December. A third son, William, born on 29 November 1698 died in 1746. A daughter, Agnes, born 5 March 1699/1700, is mentioned in the will of her uncle William in 1721, but I have found no record of either her marriage or her death. A second daughter, Magdalena, was born 11 June 1701, and, still unmarried in 1746, was charged to administer the estate of her father on the death of her brother, William. A final son, John, born on 16 June 1702, died in infancy and was buried on 2 July. Seven months later, Agnes Cleland Craige died at the age of 33; she was buried 6 February 1702/03. That left Craige in charge of a family of four, ranging in age from nineteen months to eight years; there is no record that he ever remarried.

17. "Ne autem nimium mihi adscribere, vel aliis detrahere videar, libenter agnosco, Leibnitii calculum differentialem tanta mihi in his inveniendis suppeditasse auxilia, ut sine illo haec vix assequi potuissem ea, qua optabam facilitate; quantopere solidam & sublimiorem geometriam hoc uno nobilissimo adauxerit celeberrimus eius Autor peritissimos huius aevi geometras latere non potest, & quam insignis fuerit utilitatis in dimensionibus figurarum inveniendis sequens hic tractatus sufficienter indicabit."

Titius calls attention to this passage in his preface to the 1755 edition, while at the same time he downplays or ignores similar statements of indebtedness that Craige makes to Barrow, Gregory, and Newton throughout his works. In particular, Craige's "free acknowledgment" appears in a work to which he added a letter renewing his attacks on Tschirnhaus for plagiarizing from Barrow. When Newton's quarrel with Leibniz erupted some years later, Newton on several occasions remarked that he had complained to Craige of Leibniz's plagiarism as early as 1685 (see Westfall 719; Newton, *Papers* 8:510).

18. In 1711, when Newton began to set in motion the quarrel with Leibniz over the priority of the calculus, he wrote to Sir Hans Sloane: "[Mr. Keill] shewed me some passages in those *Acta*, to justify what he said. . . . [U]pon reading them I found that I have more reason to complain of the collectors of ye mathematical papers in those *Acta* [who] everywhere insinuate to their readers that ye method of fluxions is the differential method of Mr. Leibnitz & in such a manner as if he was the true author & I had taken it from him, & give such an account of the Booke of Quadratures as if it was nothing else then an improvement of what had been found out before by Mr. Leibnitz Dr Sheen [Cheyne] & Mr. Craig" (Newton, *Correspondence* 5:117).

19. Proposition 17 makes clear that the first two chapters were written in 1696. Titius, in his 1755 edition, states (without authority) that the last four chapters were written earlier. Although there is an attempt to link the two arguments (especially at Propositions 34 and 35), the disjointed nature of the *Theology* makes it likely that the two parts were composed separately.

20. Nominated 16 May, installed 9 June (LeNeve 3:364).

3. Mathematical Principles of the *Theology*

1. A mathematical theory of probability arose as a separate field in mathematics in the decades following the Pascal-Fermat correspondence of 1654; the Newtonian calculus of fluents and the Leibnizian differential calculus arose in the years surrounding and immediately following the publication of Newton's *Principia* in 1687. I do not pretend here to offer a history of either of these two important developments, but rather to examine the mathematical principles underlying Craige's argument and relate them to these disparate, emergent fields. Various histories have offered various explanations as to why these theories emerged when they did, but they have been viewed as distinct historical events. Craige's treatise, and the confusion and controversy surrounding it, suggests that it may make sense to attend to the relationships between the concepts underlying the two theories.

For more detailed studies of the development of probability theory, see Todhunter, David, Hacking, (*Emergence;* "From the Emergence"), Garber and Zabell, Schneider, Patey, and Daston.

For more detailed studies of the development of the calculus, see Boyer (*Concepts; History*), Baron, and C. H. Edwards.

2. "Ideo res hactenus erravit incerta; nunc autem quae experimento rebellis fuerat, rationis dominium effugere non potuit: eam quippe tanta securitate in artem per geometriam reduximus, ut certitudins ejus particeps facta, jam audacter prodeat; et sic matheseos demonstrationes cum aleae incertitudine jungendo, et quae contraria videntur conciliando, abutraque nominationem suam accipiens stupendum hunc titulum jure sibi arrogat: aleae geometriae." Pascal underwent a religious conversion on the night of 23 November 1654 after which he rejected (with occasional lapses) the practice of mathematics; he is believed to have delivered the *Traité* to the Paris Academy before his conversion but after his last letter to Fermat in October 1654.

3. "Il se joue un jeu, à l'extrémité de cette distance infinie, où il arrivera croix ou pile. Que gagerez-vous?"

4. "Mais votre béatitude? Pesons le gain et la perte, en prenant croix que Dieu est. Estimons ces deux cas: si vous gagnez, vous gagnez tout; si vous perdez, vous ne perdez rien. . . . Il y a une éternité de vie et de bonheur. . . . Il y a ici une infinité de vie infiniment heureuse à gagner, un hasard de gain contre un nombre fini de hasards de perte, et ce que vous jouez est fini. Cela ôte tout parti; partout où est l'infini, et où il n'y a pas infinité de hasards de perte contre celui de gain, il n'y a point à balancer, il faut tout donner."

5. "Car il ne sert de rien de dire qu'il est incertain si on gagnera et qu'il est certain qu'on hasarde, et que l'infinie distance qui est entre la certitude de ce qu'on s'expose, et l'incertitude de ce qu'on gagnera, égale le bien fini, qu'on expose certainement, à l'infini, qui est incertain. Cela n'est pas; aussi tout joueur hasarde avec certitude pour gagner avec incertitude; et néamoins il hasarde certainement le fini pour gagner incertainement le fini, sans pécher contre la raison. Il n'y a pas infinité de distance entre cette certitude de ce qu'on s'expose et l'incertitude du gain; cela est faux. Il y a, à la vérité, infinité entre la certitude de gagner et la certitude de perdre. Mais l'incertitude de gagner est proportionnée à la certitude de ce qu'on hasarde, selon la proportion des hasards de gain et de perte. Et de là vient que, s'il y a autant de hasards d'un côté que de l'autre, le parti est à jouer égal contre égal; et alors la certitude de ce qu'on s'expose est égale à l'incertitude de gain: tant s'en faut qu'elle en soit infiniment distante. Et ainsi, notre proposition est dans une force infinie, quand il y a le fini à hasarder à un jeu où il y a pareils hasards de gain que de perte, et l'infini à gagner. Cela est démonstratif; et, si les hommes sont capables de quelque vérité, celle-là l'est.

"S'il ne fallait rien faire que pour le certain, on ne devrait rien faire pour la religion; car elle n'est pas certaine. Mais combien de choses fait-on pour l'incertain, les voyages sur mer, les batailles! Je dis donc qu'il ne faudrait rien faire du tout, car rien n'est certain; et qu'il y a plus de certitude à la religion, que non pas que nous voyions le jour de demain: car il n'est pas certain que nous voyions demain, mais il est certainement possible que nous ne le voyions pas. On n'en peut pas dire autant de la religion. Il n'est pas certain qu'elle soit; mais qui osera dire qu'il est certainement possible qu'elle ne soit pas? Or, quand on travaille pour demain, et pour l'incertain, on agit avec raison; car on doit travailler pour l'incertain, par la règle des partis qui est démontrée."

6. Newton is here responding to an anonymous review of his "Tractatus de Quadratura Curvarum." The review was in fact contributed by Leibniz himself. Whiteside presents a thorough account of this aspect of the dispute over priority in volume 8 of Newton's *Papers* (esp. 472–76).

7. In concluding his balanced evaluation of Craige's mathematical achievement in the *Theology*, Stigler makes a similar observation: "Craig was also far ahead of his time in recognizing the value of relating all variables to a common scale, choosing as his unit x, the worth of a single eyewitness's testimony. Without this convention, the different terms of his formula are incommensurable and the interpretation of the coefficients a vexed question" (21).

8. "Jamque non nisi duas alicuius momenti objectiones praevideo, quarum haec est prior: Quod non recte definiuerim tempus, quo probabilitas historiae Christi evanescere debet; cum novos probabilitatis gradus ex Prophetarum quarundam completione oriundos non consideraeurim; sed eandem in certa quadam proportione semper decrescentem acceperim. Sed responsio est facilis, haec de Christo servatore historia non aliter mihi consideranda fuit, quam qualis per aliquot saecula hactenus transmissa fuit."

9. Stigler offers a more sophisticated variant of this argument in his final analysis of Craige's calculus: "What these results show is that simple models that postulate a monotone decay of historical evidence will be insufficiently rich for practical use. The Laplace data suggest a tendency for convergence, but historians will be relieved to see it is not always towards error" (29).

10. Richard Bentley's correspondence with Newton concerning the former's Boyle Lectures reveals something of the views of those who found in Newton's *Principia* a stabilizing order arising from the doubts of the new philosophy.

11. "In philosophia experimentali, propositiones ex phaenomenis per inductionem collectae, non obstantibus contrariis hypothesibus, pro veris aut accurate aut quamproxime haberi debent, donec alia occurrerint phaenomena, per quae aut accuratiores reddantur aut exceptionibus obnoxiae."

4. Intellectual Context of the *Theology*

1. Newton's theological interests have been the subject of considerable recent study. In addition to Jacob's study of the relationship between Newtonianism and latitudinarianism, see also Manuel, Christianson (237–65), and Westfall (310–56, 804–29). Craige read and commented on the *Principia*, and we know Newton read and commented on Craige's mathematical works. Newton owned copies of all Craige's works, including the *Theology* (currently in Trinity College Library, Cambridge).

2. At the same time it echoes Spinoza: "We endeavour to bring about whatsoever we conceive to conduce to pleasure; but we endeavour to remove or destroy whatsoever we conceive to be truly repugnant thereto, or to conduce to pain" (129; pt. 3, prop. 28).

3. "Omnes homines ius habent aequale ut credantur, nis contrarium aliunde constiterit. Aequitas huius suppositionis fundatur in eo, quod res omnes eiusdem naturae iisdem praeditae sint qualitatibus naturalibus; sive hae animum sive corpus respiciunt: estque communi hominum praxi consonum, qui in quibuslibet vitae huius negotiis determinandis hominem quemlibet testem accipiunt, nisi hoc ius suum naturale aliquo modo amiserit."

4. "Temporis spatium definire, in quo Historiae Christi scriptae probabilitas evanescet."

5. "6. Probabilitas est apparentia convenientiae vel disconvenientiae duarum idearum per argumenta, quorum connexio non est constans, aut saltim talis esse non percipitur.
   7. Probabilitas naturalis est, quae deducitur ex argumentis propriae nostrae observationi aut experientiae conformibus.
   8. Probabilitas historica est, quae deducitur ex testimoniis aliorum, qui suam affirmant observationem aut experientiam."

6. See Hacking's *Emergence*, (esp. 18–31). Though he differs from Hacking on several other important issues, Patey adds further support for this earlier view of probability, while rejecting Hacking's proffered explanation of historical change. Garber and Zabell likewise dispute Hacking's explanation, in part by arguing that earlier notions of probability already contained many of the features that Hacking uses to characterize a distinctly modern conception of probability.

7. "Quid enim est Fides? Nisi illa mentis persuasio, qua propter media ex probabilitate deducta quasdam propositiones veras esse credimus. Si persuasio ex certitudine oriatur, tum non Fides sed scientia in mente producitur. Sicut enim probabilitas Fidem generat, ita etiam scientiam evertit; & e contra: Certitudo scientiam simul generat & Fidem destruit."

8. "Illi utique omnia Religionis dogmata tanquam certissima amplectentes, rem Christianismo indignam me praesiitisse putabunt, qui eius probabilitatem tantum evincere conatus suerim. Illis vero ego nihil iam habeo quod dicam, nisi quod praeiudiciis suis praeoccupati, Religionis, quam prositentur, fundamenta non accurate satis hactenus examinaverint; nec fidei, quae tantopere in sacris literis laudatur, naturam rite intellexerint."

9. "Scientiae enim adeo divinae utilitatem, non ultra angustos vitae huius limites extendi posse, absurdum plane videtur; quandoquidem per regulas geometricas omnia Naturae opera stabiliantur, ecquis dubitet easdem nos ducere ad sapientissimi Naturae Autoris cognitionem?" (00).

10. Patey tells the reader to "compare Locke's third with Coke's fourth" (24). Locke tells us in the *Essay* to consider "3. The Skill of the Witnesses" (4.15.656); Coke tells us how to evaluate the force of long-standing common report: "4. Testimony of publicke and long-lasting fame is also to be

esteemed for meanly firm" (163–64). While Locke pointedly excludes common report from those things to be considered, Coke offers no canon for evaluating the skill of witnesses, other than appeals to number and authority.

11. This is at once the strength of Patey's book and the weakness of Hacking's. Where Hacking's study tends to emphasize the suddenness of the "emergence of probability" logic in the mid-seventeenth century, Patey's study emphasizes that the emergence required no fundamental discontinuity. Both studies, however, tend too readily to equate a theoretical notion of probability logic with the broader concept of probability. In this respect, Shapiro who focuses on the historical development of the concept of probability rather than on a theoretical explanation of the emergence of probability logic, offers a more balanced guide to the actual process of historical change.

Appendix

1. Reading "se . . . ostendunt" for "se . . . ossendunt" in both 1699 and 1755 editions.

2. For Craige, following Locke's definition that probability is "the agreement or disagreement of ideas" (*Essay* 4.15.654), probability is considered the property of the reader or auditor, not of the account itself.

3. In the 1755 edition, Titius omits "the history . . . *E*."

4. The 1699 edition has a typo here, reading "EΦ" for "FΦ." Titius repeats the error in 1755.

5. Literally "duplicate ratio." I have modernized obsolete terminology such as duplicate and subduplicate for square and square root.

6. Titius omits this note in the 1755 edition.

7. The 1699 edition has here "$t = s/10$"; this error was repeated by Titius in 1755. The 1964 translation compounded the error by introducing "$t = 1/10$."

8. Titius introduced an error here in 1755, replacing "$t/8$" with "$10t/8$"; Titius is followed by the 1964 translation, but since Craige ignores the fractions immediately below, there is no impact on the argument.

9. Craige's syntax here may have confused many of his readers: "Necesse est, ut Christus veniat, antequam elabantur anni 1454." The 1964 translation, ignoring the commas, renders this as, "It is necessary that Christ come before 1454 years elapse." As the subsequent context makes clear, however, Craige's interest is anti-Apocalyptic, designed to show that the world cannot end for at least another 1454 years. One of the ironies surrounding the *Theology* is that it is frequently characterized as typifying the millenarian frenzy it was intended to oppose.

10. See note 8, above.

11. Craige here had "*V*"; Titius corrected it in 1755.

12. Literally "multiplied or submultiplied ratio," obsolete terminology for exponential functions where an integral exponent is described as multiplied and a fractional exponent is described as submultiplied.

13. In 1699, Craige incorrectly had 955125/354662; Titus corrected his error in 1755. Craige seems to have made his mistake while reducing fractions. His formula should yield:

$$[(25^3 - 7^3)/7^3] \div [(13^3 - 5^3)/5^3], \text{ or}$$
$$[(25^3 - 7^3)/7^3] \cdot [5^3/(13^3 - 5^3)].$$

This equals $(15282/343) \cdot (125/2072)$. This can be reduced to $(7641 \cdot 125)/(343 \cdot 1036)$, which yields the correct result. Craige's answer may be obtained if one reduces this fraction to $(7641 \cdot 125)/(343 \cdot 1034)$.

14. Both 1699 and 1755 editions have "*EB*."

WORKS CITED

Administrations of the Estate of John Craig. PROB 6/107. November, 1731; June, 1746. Public Record Office. London, England.

Arber, Edward. *The Term Catalogues, 1688–1709*. Vol. 3. London, 1906.

Arbuthnot, John. *Of the Laws of Chance*. London, 1692.

Bacon, Francis. *The Works of Francis Bacon*. Ed. James Spedding, Robert L. Ellis, and Douglas D. Heath. 15 vols. London: Longmans, 1857.

Ball, W. W. Rouse. *A History of the Study of Mathematics at Cambridge*. Cambridge: Cambridge UP, 1889.

Baron, Margaret E. *The Origins of the Infinitesimal Calculus*. New York: Pergamon, 1969.

Barrow, Isaac. *Geometrical Lectures*. Ed. J. M. Child. Chicago: Open Court, 1916.

Berkeley, George. *Works*. Ed. Alexander Campbell Fraser. 4 vols. Oxford: Clarendon, 1901.

Bishop, Morris. *Pascal, The Life of Genius*. New York: Reynal, 1936.

Boyer, Carl. *Concepts of the Calculus*. New York: Hafner, 1949.

———. *History of Mathematics*. New York: Wiley, 1968.

Bradford, Samuel. *The Credibility of the Christian Religion*. London, 1700.

Brewster, Sir David. *Memoirs of the Life, Writings, and Discoveries of Sir Isaac Newton*. 2 vols. Edinburgh, 1855.

Burnet, Gilbert. *History of My Own Times*. London, 1724.

———. Letter to John Colbatch. 1 Jan. 1701/2. Sloane MSS. 22,908. British Library, London, England.

Burnet, Thomas. *The Letters of Thomas Burnet to George Duckett 1712–1722*. Ed. David Nichol Smith. Oxford: Roxburghe Club, 1914.

Cajori, Florian. *History of Mathematics*. New York: MacMillan, 1919.

Chester, J. L. *Westminster Abbey Registers*. London, 1876.

Chester, J. L., and G. J. Armytage. *Marriage Licenses—London, 1611–1828*. 2 vols. London, 1887.

Cheyne, George. *Philosophical Principles of Natural and Revealed Religion*. London, 1715.

Christianson, Gale. *In the Presence of the Creator*. New York: MacMillan, 1984.

Clarke, Samuel. *A Discourse on the Evidence of Natural and Revealed Religion*. London, 1705.

Cohen, I. Bernard. *Introduction to Newton's* Principia. Cambridge: Harvard UP, 1978.

Coke, Zachary. *The Art of Logick; or the Entire Body of Logick in English*. London, 1654.

Craige, John. *De Calculo Fluentium*. London, 1718.

———. Letter to David Gregory. 11 Apr. 1695. Tanner ms. Folio 20. Dept. of Western Manuscripts, Bodleian Library, Oxford University, Oxford, England.

———. *Methodus Figurarum Lineis Rectis et Curvis Comprehensarum Quadraturas Determinandi*. London, 1685.

———. *Theologiae Christianae Principia Mathematica*. London, 1699.

———. *Theologiae Christianae Principia Mathematica*. Ed. J. Daniel Titius. Leipzig, 1755.

————. *Tractatus Mathematicus de Figurarum Curvilinearum Quadraturis & Locis Geometricis*. London, 1693.

"Craig's Rules of Historical Evidence." *History and Theory* Beiheft 4 (1964).

Daston, Lorraine. *Classical Probability in the Enlightenment*. Princeton UP, 1988.

David, F. N. *Games, Gods, and Gambling*. New York: Hafner, 1962.

DeMoivre, Abraham. *The Doctrine of Chances*. London, 1712.

Ditton, Humphrey. *Discourse Concerning the Resurrection of Jesus Christ*. London: J. Darby, 1714.

Edwards, C. H. *The Historical Development of the Calculus*. New York: Springer-Verlag, 1979.

Edwards, John. *Some New Discoveries of the Uncertainty, Deficiency, and Corruption of Human Knowledge and Learning*. London, 1714.

Foucault, Michel. *The Order of Things*. New York: Vintage, 1970.

Foxcroft, Helen. *A Life of Gilbert Burnet, Bishop of Salisbury*. Cambridge: Cambridge UP, 1907.

Garber, Daniel, and Sandy Zabell. "On the Emergence of Probability." *Archive for the History of Exact Sciences* 21 (1979): 33–53.

Gillingham Christenings, Marriages and Burials. Dorset County Record Office. County Hall. Dorchester, England.

Greenblatt, Stephen. "Introduction." *Genre* 15.1–2 (1982): 3–6.

Gregory, David. Notebooks. Christ Church College Library, Oxford University, Oxford, England.

Guerrini, Anita. "The Tory Newtonians: Gregory, Pitcairne and Their Circle." *Journal of British Studies* 25.3 (1986): 288–312.

Hacking, Ian. *The Emergence of Probability*. Cambridge: Cambridge UP, 1975.

————. "From the Emergence of Probability to the Erosion of Determinism." *Probabilistic Thinking, Thermodynamics, and the Interaction of the History and Philosophy of Science*. Ed. J. Hintikka, et al. Vol. 2. Dordrecht: Reidel, 1981. 105–23.

Hall, A. Rupert. *Philosophers at War: The Quarrel Between Newton and Leibniz*. Cambridge: Cambridge UP, 1980.

Halley, Edmond. "An Estimate on the degrees of mortality of mankind, drawn from the curious tables of the birth and funerals at the city of Breslaw; with an attempt to ascertain the price of annuities upon lives." *Philosophical Transactions of the Royal Society of London* 17 (1693): 596–610.

Historical Manuscript Commission Report on MSS of the Duke of Portland. 9 vols. London: Eyre, 1899–1931.

Historical Manuscript Commission Report on MSS of the Duke of Roxburgh. London: Eyre, 1894.

Hooke, Robert. "Hooke's Diary." *Early Science in Oxford*. Ed. R. T. Gunther. Vol. 10. Oxford, 1935.

[Hooper, George.] "A Calculation of the Credibility of Human Testimony." *Philosophical Transactions of the Royal Society of London* 21 (1699): 359–65.

Hooper, George. *Works*. Oxford, 1757.

Houtteville, Abbé. *La Religion Chrétienne Prouvée par les Faits*. Paris, 1722.

Hume, David. *Treatise of Human Nature*. Oxford: Oxford UP, 1955.

Jacob, Margaret C. *Newtonianism and the English Revolution, 1689–1720*. Ithaca: Cornell UP, 1976.

Keynes ms. 132. Dated 7 Apr. 1727. King's College Library, Cambridge University.

LeNeve, John. *Fasti Ecclesiae Anglicanae*. Ed. T. Duffus Hardy. 3 vols. Oxford: Oxford UP, 1834.

Locke, John. *An Essay Concerning Human Understanding*. Ed. P. H. Nidditch. Oxford: Clarendon, 1975.

————. *The Reasonableness of Christianity*. London, 1690.

[Lubbock and Drinkwater]. "On Probability." *Jones on Annuities and Reversionary Payments with Treatise on Probability*. Vol. 2. London, 1844.

Manuel, Frank. *The Religion of Isaac Newton*. Cambridge: Harvard UP, 1974.

Montmort, Phillipe. *Essai D'Analyse*. Paris, 1710.

Newton, Isaac. *The Correspondence of Isaac Newton*. Ed. Henry Turnbull, A. Rupert Hall, and Laura Tilling. 7 vols. Cambridge: Cambridge UP, 1959–78.

————. *The Mathematical Papers of Isaac Newton*. Ed. D. T. Whiteside. 8 vols. Cambridge: Cambridge UP, 1967–81.

————. *Opticks*. New York: Dover, 1952.

————. *Philosophiae Naturalis Principia Mathematica*. Ed. Alexandre Koyré and I. Bernard Cohen. 2 vols. Harvard UP, 1972.

Palter, Robert. "Newton and the Inductive Method." *The Annus Mirabilis of Sir Isaac Newton, 1666–1966*. Ed. Robert Palter. Cambridge: MIT, 1970. 244–57.

Parish Registers for St. James, Clerkenwell. "Burials." London: Mitchell, 1884–93.

Pascal, Blaise. *Oeuvres Complêtes*. Ed. Louis Lafuma. Paris: Macmillan, 1963.

————. *Pensées*. Paris: Garnier Frères, 1964.

Patey, Douglas Lane. *Probability and Literary Form: Philosophic Theory and Literary Practice in the Augustan Age*. Cambridge: Cambridge UP, 1984.

Peirce, C. S. *Writings of Charles S. Peirce*. Vol. 3. Bloomington: Indiana UP, 1986.

Phipson, Sidney L. *The Law of Evidence*. Ed. J. H. Buzzard. 12th ed. London: Sweet, 1976.

Pope, Alexander. *The Twickenham Edition of the Works of Alexander Pope*. Ed. John Butt, et al. 11 vols. Yale UP, 1939–69.

Raphson, Joseph. *History of Fluxions*. London, 1715.

Schneider, Ivo. "Why Do We Find the Origin of a Calculus of Probability in the Seventeenth Century?" *Probabilistic Thinking, Thermodynamics, and the Interaction of the History and Philosophy of Science*. Ed. J. Hintikka, et al. Vol. 2. Dordrecht: Reidel, 1981: 3–24.

Shapin, Steven. "Social Uses of Science." *The Ferment of Knowledge*. Ed. G. S. Rousseau and Roy Porter. Cambridge: Cambridge UP, 1980. 93–142.

Shapiro, Barbara. *Probability and Certainty in Seventeenth-Century England*. Princeton UP, 1983.

Spinoza, Baruch. *The Ethics*. Trans. R. H. M. Elwes. New York: J. Simon, 1981.

Stephen, Sir Leslie, and Sir Sidney Lee, eds. *Dictionary of National Biography*. 22 vols. 1949–50.

Stigler, Stephen. "John Craig and the Probability of History: From the Death of Christ to the Birth of Laplace." Technical Report No. 165. Dept. of Statistics. U of Chicago, 1985.

Stone, Lawrence. *The Family, Sex and Marriage in England, 1500–1800*. New York: Harper, 1977.

Tindal, Matthew. *Christianity as Old as Creation*. London, 1730.

Todhunter, Isaac. *A History of the Mathematical Theory of Probability from Pascal to Laplace*. New York: Chelsea, 1949.

Warburton, William. *The Divine Legation of Moses*. London, 1738.

Westfall, Richard S. *Never at Rest*. Cambridge: Cambridge UP, 1980.

Will of William Craig, proved 1721. PROB 11/578f. 353Rh–354Lh. Public Record Office. London, England.

Wotton, William. *Reflections on Ancient and Modern Learning*. London, 1694.

INDEX

Abduction, 29, 31. *See also* Induction; Newtonian method
Allix, Peter, 12
Ancients and Moderns, 14
Arbuthnot, John, 13, 19; *Of the Laws of Chance,* 22

Bacon, Francis, 29
Ball, W. W. Rouse, 1
Barrow, Isaac, 9–10, 23, 26, 28, 30
Bayes, Thomas, 27
Bentley, Richard, 12, 32
Berkeley, George, Bp., 4
Bonde, Gustave, Comte de, 6
Boyle, Robert, 12
Bradford, Samuel, 3, 12
Brewster, Sir David, 15
Burnet, Gilbert, Bp., 8, 11, 14, 18; Burnet, Gilbert (2d son), 11–12, 17; Burnet, Thomas (3d son), 8, 16–17; Burnet, William (1st son), 14

Cajori, Florian, 1
Calculus of fluents, xvi, 6, 9, 19, 22, 28–29
Campbell, Colin, 8–9
Cheyne, Dr. George, 15, 23
Clarke, Samuel, xv, 3–4
Cleland, John, 12
Clemm, Henri Guillaume, 6
Cohen, I. Bernard, 10
Coke, Zachary, 41
Colbatch, John, 12
Conceptualist probability, 25
Conduitt, John, 9, 32
Craig, John (Scottish reformer), 8
Craige, John: Agnes (née Cleland, wife), 12; Agnes (daughter), 17; ancestry, 8; contributes to G. Cheyne's *Philosophical Principles,* 16; contributes to W. Wotton's *Reflections,* 14, 19; "Craig's Rules of Historical Evidence," 1; *De Calculo Fluentium,* 9, 16;

elected F.R.S., 15; "faith" defined, 7; Gilbert (son), 12; James (father), 8, 11; Magdalen (daughter), 17–18; memoir of Newton, 9; *Methodus Figurarum,* 8, 10; *Tractatus Mathematicus,* 12; tutors mathematics, 14; William (brother), 8, 11–12, 14, 17–18; William (son), 18
Craige, Mary (wife of William), 17

Daston, Lorraine, 2–3
DeMoivre, Abraham, 15, 19, 22
Deslandes, Monsieur, 15
Ditton, Humphrey, xv, 4, 27, 39–41, 43–45
Doctrine of chances, 39. *See also* Probability, logic
Duality, 25, 42
Duckett, George, 16–17
Durnford, 11–12, 15

Edwards, C. H., 28
Edwards, John, 4, 27, 35, 41

Fagot, Anne M., xvi
Fermat, Pierre, 19–20
Finch, Mary, 14
Foucault, Michel, xvi
Fox, Francis, 12
Francis, Convers, 3
Freek, Tom, 17

George I, 16
Gillingham Major, 11, 15, 17
Gloucester, Duke of, 14
Greenblatt, Stephen, xviii
Gregory, David, 8–9, 13, 22–23
Gregory, James, 8
Grier, Brown, 3

Hacking, Ian, xvi–xvii, 1, 19, 25, 29, 35, 37–39, 41–44
Halifax, Marquis of, 14
Hall, A. Rupert, 10
Halley, Edmond, 8, 14–15, 19
Harley, Robert, Earl of Oxford, 15

Hermann, Jacques, 6
Historical faith, 34–35
Hoadly, John, 12
Hofmann, J. E., 28
Hogarth, William, 17
Hooke, Robert, 8, 11
Hooper, George, 3, 23–26
Houtteville, Abbe, 4, 27
Howe, Sir Richard, 15
Hume, David, xv, 5, 27, 29–31

Induction, 29, 31, 39, 42, 44. *See also*
  Probability, logic

James II, 11

Kaestner, Abraham-Gotthelf, 6
Knittel, Francois-Antoine, 6

Langhorn, Richard, 43
Latitudinarian, 12
Leibniz, Gottfried Wilhelm, 6, 9–10, 12–
  13, 23, 26
Leibnizian notation, xvi, 9, 23
Locke, John, xv, xvii, 2, 7, 26, 32–41,
  43–45
Log likelihood ratio, 19, 24
Longitude, the problem of, 17
Lubbock and Drinkwater, xvii, 1–2, 7,
  30, 43

MacLaurin, Colin, 8
Marlborough, Duke of, 14
Materialist probability, 25
Montmort, Phillipe de, xv, 6, 26

Newton, Isaac, xv, xviii, 6–10, 12–13,
  15, 17, 22–23, 26, 28, 30–32
Newtonian dot notation, xvi, 9, 23
Newtonian method, 29–30, 39, 43–44.
  See also Abduction
North, Lord Chief Justice, 42–43
Nottingham, Earl of, 14

Oates, Titus, 42

Pascal, Blaise, xvi, 7, 19, 31, 35; "the
  wager," xvii–xviii, 2, 20–21, 26, 30,
  33, 37, 39, 43–44
Patey, Douglas Lane, xvi, 1, 3, 37–39,
  41, 43–44

Peerage bill, 16
Peirce, C. S., xvii, 25, 27, 29. *See also*
  Abduction; Induction
Petersen, Johann Wilhelm, 3
Pitcairne, Archibald, 8–9
Poleni, Giovanni, 6
Pope, Alexander, xv, 5, 26
Potterne, 11, 13
Price, Richard, 27
Probability, of Christianity, 4, 7, 26–28,
  34–35; conflicting notions of, 25–26,
  42–44; Lockean, 33–37; logic, 19, 29,
  43–44; mathematical theory of, xvi, 2–
  3, 7, 19, 22–23, 25, 29, 31, 35; moral
  applications of, 20–22; of testimony,
  1, 4, 6, 19, 23–24, 27, 34, 38–41, 44

Raphson, Joseph, 23
Roxburgh, John Ker, 1st Duke of, 14,
  16; Mary Finch Ker (wife), 14; Robert
  Ker, 2d Duke (son), 14

St. James, Clerkenwell, 15, 18
Scott, J. F., 26
Shapin, Steven, xviii
Shapiro, Barbara, xvi, 42
South Sea Bubble, 16
Speake, Mr., 16
Stafford, Earl of, 42
Stanhope, James, 16
Stigler, Stephen, xviii, 2–3, 19, 24
Swift, Jonathan, 12, 14

Tindal, Matthew, xv, 4, 7
Titius, J. Daniel, 6
Todhunter, Isaac, 3
Tschirnhaus, D., 10, 23

Upwey, 11

Venn, J. A., 25

Wallis, John, 26
Walpole, 16
Warburton, William, xv, 4–5
Westminster Abbey, 11, 14, 17
Whiteside, D. T., 10, 28
William III, 11
Wotton, William, 12, 14, 38

RICHARD NASH RECEIVED HIS PH.D. IN 1986 FROM THE UNIVERSITY OF VIRGINIA. He is an assistant professor of English at Indiana University, and he is currently at work on a book on the epistemological satire of Swift and Pope.